Top 25 locator map
(continues on inside
back cover)

CW01095935

CityPack
Orlando *Top 25*

If you have any comments
or suggestions for this guide
you can contact the editor at
Citypack@TheAA.com

AA Publishing
Find out more about AA Publishing and the wide range
of travel publications and services the AA provides by
visiting our website at *www.TheAA.com/bookshop*

About This Book

ORGANIZATION

This guide is divided into six chapters:

- Planning Ahead, Getting There
- Living Orlando–Orlando Now, Orlando Then, Time to Shop, Out and About, Walks, Orlando by Night
- Orlando's Top 25 Sights
- Orlando's Best–best of the rest
- Where To–detailed listings of restaurants, hotels, stores and nightlife
- Travel Facts–practical information

In addition, easy-to-read side panels provide extra facts and snippets, highlights of places to visit and invaluable practical advice.

The colors of the tabs on the page corners match the colors of the triangles aligned with the chapter names on the contents page opposite.

MAPS

The fold-out map in the wallet at the back of this book is a comprehensive street plan of Orlando. The first (or only) grid reference given for each attraction refers to this map. **The Top 25 locator map** found on the inside front and back covers of the book itself is for quick reference. It shows the Top 25 Sights, described on pages 26–50, which are clearly plotted by number (**1**–**25**, not page number) across the region. The second map reference given for the Top 25 Sights refers to this map.

Contents

Planning Ahead

WHEN TO GO

Orlando's attractions stay open throughout the year. For the best weather, visit during October and November, March and April, when the weather is warm but the air is not too humid. The quietest times at the theme parks are September until Thanksgiving (third Thursday in November). The busiest times are around the major holidays and June to August.

AVERAGE DAILY MAXIMUM TEMPERATURES

JAN	FEB	MAR	APR	MAY	JUN	JUL	AUG	SEP	OCT	NOV	DEC
72°F	73°F	77°F	81°F	81°F	86°F	90°F	90°F	86°F	82°F	77°F	72°F
22°C	23°C	25°C	27°C	27°C	30°C	32°C	32°C	30°C	28°C	25°C	22°C

Orlando sits at the northern belt of the subtropical climate zone.
Spring has warm days. Rain and short storms are possible at any time, all year round.
Summer (Jun–Sep) are extremely hot and humid with regular thunderstorms. This is also hurricane season. Direct hits from big storms are rare, but the area suffered three in 2004.
Fall offers cooler temperatures and quieter weather. Nights are still warm.
Winter has average daytime temperatures in the low 70s Fahrenheit. (early 20s Centigrade), though be aware that temperatures may drop much further. Pack a sweater!

WHAT'S ON

February *Silver Springs Rodeo* in Kissimmee is the biggest cowboy gathering in Florida with bull and bronco riding contests.
Arts Festival: the Bach Festival Society hosts concerts at Rollins College, Winter Park.
Four weekends leading up to *Mardi Gras* (and the nights themselves) turn Universal CityWalk into party central.
March The *Bay Hill Invitational* golf tournament at the Bay Hill Club is hosted by Arnold Palmer.

Watch *baseball spring training* with the Atlanta Braves at Disney's Wild World of Sport and the Houston Astros at Osceola Heritage Park, Kissimmee.
April *Orlando Film Festival.*
May *Orlando International Fringe Festival*: 10 days of irreverent comedy performances.
July *WLOQ Jazz Jams*: the open-air concerts at Winter Park run through August.
October See *Silver Springs Rodeo* (part 2) at Kissimmee and the *FUNAI Classic* golf tournament at Walt Disney

World® Resort.
Halloween: the weekend leading up to the event turns CityWalk into a partying "ghoul town."
The *International Food Festival* at Epcot® runs into early November.
November The *Festival of the Masters* is an arts festival at Downtown Disney West Side.
December Disney's Magic Kingdom® is turned into a *Christmas* wonderland with festive decorations, concerts, special parades and fireworks displays.

ORLANDO ONLINE
The Internet is a goldmine of information about Orlando. You can check what is going on at the theme parks and make bookings online.

www.orlandoinfo.com
The official website of the Orlando Convention and Visitors Bureau with information on what to do and where to go. Links to websites to book discounted accommodations. You can also order booklets and buy the MagiCard.

www.floridakiss.com
Kissimmee's official website with information on attractions in the downtown area and along I-192 (Irlo Bronson Memorial Highway). Book discount hotels through the site.

www.visitseminole.com
Official Seminole County Convention and Visitors Bureau, with information on attractions in Orlando's most natural region, plus "what's on" and hotel information.

www.disney.go.com
Disney's official website with information on all parks and resorts. You can book accommodations and restaurant tables.

www.allearsnet.com
An easy-to-navigate unofficial Disney site that has lots of practical tips and background on enjoying Walt Disney World® Resort.

www.universalorlando.com
Universal Orlando's official site. A good overview, with the ability to book hotel rooms and restaurants. Useful to find out what's happening at Universal CityWalk®.

www.nps.gov
Official website of the American National Park Service with details on how to visit all the parks and background information on animals, birds and natural environments. Park guidelines for visitors are also posted.

CYBERCAFÉS

Bad Ass Café
✉ 8554 International Drive
☎ 407/226-8673
🕐 Daily 10–10
💻 $8 per hour (can be used over 48 hours)

Cybershack Café
✉ 6438 International Drive
☎ 407/363-1443
🕐 Daily 8am–midnight
💻 $8 per hour (can be used over 48 hours)

Guinevere's Coffee House and Gallery
✉ 37–39 South Magnolia Avenue
☎ 407/992-1200
🕐 Mon–Fri 8am–midnight, Sat noon–midnight
💻 $3 per hour

World of Coffee
✉ Lake Buena Vista Factory Stores, 15533 South Apopka Vineland Road
☎ 407/256-6784
🕐 Mon–Sat 10–9, Sun 10–6
💻 $8 per hour (can be used over 48 hours)

Getting There

ENTRY REQUIREMENTS

All foreign visitors require a valid passport, except Canadians, who need proof of citizenship. Citizens of the following countries can arrive in the US for less than 90 days for business or pleasure under the Visa Waiver Scheme provided that they have a machine-readable passport and at least six months validity on their passport – Australia, Germany, Ireland, New Zealand and the UK (plus most other EU countries). Others should consult the American Embassy in their own country for visa requirements. Regulations can change. Always check before you travel.

MONEY

The unit of currency is the dollar (=100 cents). Bills come in denominations of $1, $5, $10, $20, $50 and $100. Coins are $1, 50¢, 25¢ (quarter), 10¢ (dime), 5¢ (nickel) and 1¢ (penny).

$10

$50

ARRIVING

There are direct flights from continental Europe to Orlando's international airport, but most transatlantic flights are routed via London. Airport facilities include an information desk, a small of number shops (including a pharmacy), bureaux de change, restaurants and car rental.

BY AIR

The primary international airport is Orlando International (MCO) ☎ 407/825-2001, 6.5 miles (10.5km) southeast of the city. The downtown journey takes about 20 minutes, International Drive can be reached in 30 minutes and Walt Disney World® Resort in 45 minutes.

Lynx public bus services 11, 41, 42 and 51 serve the airport, but none travel directly to the main tourist areas.

An airport shuttle can be booked to most hotels in the tourist areas. Mears ☎ 407/432-5566 is the major supplier.

Adult prices to International Drive are $25 one-way, to the Disney area $29 one-way, and downtown Orlando $25 one-way.

Walt Disney World® Resort operates a free shuttle, Disney's Magical Express, from Orlando International Airport to all Disney Resort Hotels, except the Walt Disney World Swan and Dolphin hotel and the Downtown Disney Resort area hotels. You will travel directly to your hotel and they will collect all bags at the airport and deliver them to your room. This service is available only to Walt Disney World® Resort guests.

If you're not staying at a Disney hotel, take a taxi from the airport: Yellow/City Cab (☎ 407/699-9999 or 407/422-2222) is a reliable company. Daytime fares per cab are about $30 to Universal Studios and International Drive, $50 to Epcot® (slightly more to the Magic Kingdom area) and $27 to the downtown area.

The secondary airport for the city is Sanford International (SFB), 18 miles (11km) northwest of the downtown area (☎ 407/585-4000). There are flights to smaller American cities and Sanford accommodates charter flights from the UK and Western Europe.

Journey time to the downtown area is 45 minutes. It is an hour to International Drive and at least 1 hour 15 minutes to the Disney area. Lynx bus 33 services the airport, connecting with Seminole Center just south of Sanford and 10 miles (17km) north of downtown Orlando.

The taxi service from the airport (☎ 407/422-2222) has prices to downtown from about $58, to International Drive from $77 and to Walt Disney World® Resort from $100.

BY BUS

Greyhound services link Orlando with the rest of the United States. There are stations at Downtown (✉ 555 North John Young Parkway, ☎ 407/292-3440), Sanford (✉ 1300 West Airport Boulevard, ☎ 407/688-9725) and Kissimmee (✉ 103 East Dakin Avenue, ☎ 407/847-3911). For information on routes and costs consult **www.**greyhound.com.

Taxi fares (see above) from the station to the Downtown area are $10, to International Drive $18 and to the Disney area $41.

BY TRAIN

The vast Amtrak passenger network has stations in downtown Orlando (✉ 1400 Sligh Boulevard, Winter Park; ✉ West Morse Boulevard, Sanford; ✉ 800 Persimmon Street, and Kissimmee ✉ 111 Dakin Street). Customer service can be contacted on ☎ 1 800/872-7245; **www.**amtrak.com.

Taxi fares (see above) from the station to International Drive $23, to the Disney area $44.

INSURANCE

It is vital to have comprehensive medical insurance as all treatment is chargeable and costs can be high. It is also advisable to have insurance for loss or theft of your property and documents and to cover any travel delays or cancellations. Numerous insurance companies sell combined insurance packages for either a single trip or on an annual multitrip basis.

VISITORS WITH DISABILITIES

Facilities for visitors with disabilities are generally excellent in Orlando, with toilet facilities, ramps and automatic doors or special entrances on all public buildings, shopping malls and tourist attractions. Most public walkways feature ramps at street intersections. All public transport buses have wheelchair access. Most hotels have some rooms specifically designed for disabled guests. The majority of organizations have TTY (Text Telephone) telephone services for the deaf or hard of hearing and many have Braille information for visitors with visual impairment.

Living
Orlando

Orlando Now

Above: a neon sign for Universal Studios Florida

Forty years ago, few people had heard of Orlando. A city at the center of citrus and cattle country, it barely registered on the radar of the North American people, let alone across the seas in Europe and Australia. The year that changed everything was 1966. The Walt Disney jamboree had come to town, staking a major claim in the form of 27,000 acres (10,925ha) of Florida scrub. A "gold rush" atmosphere descended on the city. Orlando was to be the new tourism capital of the country and smart investors were going to get a slice of the pie.

In fact, Walt Disney did more than simply set the ball rolling; he redefined the tourism and leisure market for the rest of the century and into the

IMAGINEERS

• More than decorators, more than graphics experts, "imagineers" are a new breed of designer whose job it is to take the basic skeleton of an idea for a new show or ride then combine the simplest visual effects with complex computer effects, laser technology and the finest quality materials for sets and landscaping to make everything look and feel just right. It is this unswerving attention to myriad tiny details that makes Disney and Universal parks the incredible experiences they are.

Far left: *traditional houses in Thornton Park*
Left: *meeting cartoon characters at Universal Studios Islands of Adventure*
Below: *Downtown Orlando*

GREEN ROOTS...

● It's still possible to find an unspoiled natural Orlando, remote from the artificial 21st-century pleasures. Ruled by water, this landscape is thousands of years old and supports a complicated and sensitive ecosystem where three animals reign supreme. No, not Mickey, Donald and Goofy, but the brown bear, the Florida cougar and the American alligator.

...AND THE CITY'S ROOTS

● To get a feel of how Orlando would have looked 150 years ago head north to Longwood. The tiny enclave of the historic district has a collection of late Victorian buildings. They're not grand enough to be called mansions but are handsome all the same.

third millennium. And of course he changed this ingenuous regional capital forever with the simple signature on a real estate deal. Today Orlando parks occupy six out of the top ten theme parks in America (by visitor count) and tourist numbers have skyrocketed from a mere 660,000 in 1970 to 40 million in 1999. Experts suggest that the 50 million mark could be broken in 2005.

Unlike many destinations, people are pretty sure what they are arriving in Orlando for. They expect to have fun; nothing cerebral, no heavy culture, just unadulterated pleasure. And the city works hard to make fun seem effortless.

Above: a sign for Toon Lagoon at Universal Studios Islands of Adventure

Thousands of workers earning a living here aren't called "employees" they're "cast members"; an army of people that bring Cinderella, Peter Pan, Scooby Doo and Shrek to life. Always cheerful and wearing a constant smile they strive to turn the clichéd mantra "have a nice day" into reality.

For many visitors, Orlando isn't so much a city as a portal. It's a departure point from where they can be transported anywhere but to central Florida, reveling in Africa or Asia, diving head-long into Tomorrowland or walking backward through time in Jurassic Park. It's a land of "Lands" created with such precision by "imagi-neers" that normal frames of reference are suspended. The city grows ever stronger on "the wow factor" – fastest, highest, deepest, longest – an attraction doesn't even make it on to the tourist "must do" list if it doesn't come with its own superlative, or preferably a string of them.

The statistics are impressive: there are 95 attrac-tions (most under the category "family fun"), 113,000 hotel rooms, 5,100 restaurants and over 100 nightlife venues that all run the full

GETTING DOWN TO BUSINESS

• Orlando's Convention Center, on International Drive, is the second largest in the United States with 2.1 million sq ft (189,000sq m) of exhibition space. The city welcomes over 5 million convention visitors every year with everyone from surgeons to pet food purveyors getting together for their industry powwow.

gamut of taste and budget. And visitors to the city come from all walks of life. In fact, such a representative sample of American society vacations here that national chains use Orlando's captive market to soft-launch new recipes and room styling. So much that's innovative in the

Above: Orange County Convention Center

GETTING AROUND

• Orlando cannot be described as compact and to make the most of what the city has to offer, you really need to rent a car. It's 15 miles (24km) south from downtown to the Disney parks or to Kissimmee and 10 miles (16km) to International Drive. Head north and it's 3 miles (5km) to Winter Park, 12 miles (20km) to Wekiwa Springs and 20 miles (32km) to the Central Florida Zoo.

• If you don't want to rent a car, then a stay on International Drive will mean (usually) free shuttle bus access to the major parks (30 minutes to Disney, 15 minutes to Universal) and I-Ride for the attractions along the Drive itself.

• If you stay at a Disney or Universal hotel and only intend to visit the resort parks, complimentary transport will be available.

Above: Downtown Orlando
Above right: seeking shade
from the sun at a café table

American hospitality industry starts here and is taken up by destinations elsewhere.

Any other city would have buckled under the strain of this remarkable transformation, yet on the surface there seems remarkably little stress. Clever planning has played its part, particularly around the theme parks, but then the city had a clean slate to start the process. Traffic jams on major routes are a daily fact of life but no more so than in Cleveland, Manchester or Bonn.

The effects on the environment, however, are a different matter. Hundreds of thousands of acres of land around Orlando have been snapped up for development, putting pressure on the fragile ecosystems on which Florida's diverse native wildlife depends.

With the magnetic pull of the theme parks so strong, it's amazing that the city manages any visibility at all, but there is life beyond the shadow of the "mouse." Downtown Orlando is diminutive when compared with other cities of its stature, with only a scattering of skyscrapers to define the corporate enclave. These are inter-

THE FIRST THEME PARK

● In 1895, following the big freeze, John B. Steinmetz converted his disused citrus-packing plant into a skating rink, toboggan track and bathhouse. It proved to be highly successful and drew crowds of locals and tourists.

spersed with low-level, early-20th-century brick edifices, carefully primped and preened under the proud title "historic district." Thornton Park, around central Lake Eola and its park, is a splendid area. City dwellers there have tree-lined cobbled avenues, painted picket fences and porches on which to spend balmy evenings. With resident ballet, opera and orchestra companies, plus some well-respected collections of North and South American artifacts, they also enjoy a vibrant arts scene. Because land was so cheap Orlando spread outward, not up, and it stretches for miles, an agglomeration of modern suburbs mostly built since the 1980s. Winter Park to the north of downtown is the city's most picturesque and enchanting neighborhood with a history dating back more than a hundred years, excellent museums for those who need a culture fix and a great café scene.

If fun is what you're looking for then Orlando is one place you shouldn't miss. There are enough thrills here to fill several vacations. But look beyond the obvious and you may be surprised by what you find in one of the 21st-century's most typecast cities.

Above: International Drive
Above left: Big Tree Park

WHAT'S IN A NAME?

● Aaron Jermyn, beneficiary of the Armed Occupation Act, settled here in 1843, founding Jermyn on the site of Fort Gatlin. In 1857 Jermyn became Orlando. Some say that the name pays tribute to Orlando Reeves, killed defending the fort in 1835. Others say that local Judge Deeds named the town after the character in Shakespeare's "As You Like It," one of his favorite plays.

15

Orlando Then

Above: a painting by John F. Clymer (1845) shows American soldiers in boats and Native Americans hiding by the shore during the Seminole Wars in Florida
Above right: orange groves were planted in the 1850s

THE SENATOR

The oldest cypress tree in the United States is found in the Orlando metropolitan area. Christened "The Senator" it is estimated to be about 3,500 years old. It was a sapling during the age of the great Egyptian pharaohs and saw dozens of Timucuan generations when in its prime. The sturdy trunk is 120ft (36m) high but the Senator lost its canopy a couple of decades ago during a hurricane.
✚ Off map
✉ Big Tree Park, General Hutchinson Parkway, Longwood

c10,000BC The first humans settle in the St. John's River area of Central Florida.

c500BC Timucuan (➤ 44) tribes arrive.

1513 Europeans, in the form of the Spanish, bring cattle, and diseases that wipe out the Timucuan.

1500–late 1700s Central Florida remains mainly untouched by European settlement.

Late 1700s Native American Seminoles, pushed south by European colonization, settle in the area. At the same time settlers descended from Scottish and Irish immigrants and known as "Crackers," move inland.

1819 The United States receives Florida from Spain as debt repayment.

1835 The Seminole lose the 2nd Seminole Indian War and are forced from the region.

1842 The Armed Occupation Act boosts white settlement of Central Florida.

1843 Orlando established (➤ 15). Florida becomes a state two years later.

1850s Citrus groves are established. They, along with cattle, form the staple industries in the region.

1856 Orlando becomes the county seat of Orange County.

1870 The St. John's River – from Jacksonville down through central Florida to Orlando – is the busiest waterway south of the Hudson. Orlando becomes a major market place and shipment point.

1882 The South Florida Railroad reaches Orlando and trade booms.

1894–5 The "Big Freeze" destroys the citrus groves in Central Florida.

1896 The suburb of Sanford swaps citrus for celery to become "celery capital of the world."

1913 Sanford splits from Orlando to become capital of Seminole County.

1943 The 172 military installations in Florida include Orlando Air Base.

Post-war Orlando's aerospace industry boasts Cape Canaveral space center.

1966 Walt Disney (top) buys 27,000 acres of land to the southwest of the city for his vision: Walt Disney World®.

Dec 1966 Death of Walt Disney – his plans are continued by brother Roy.

1971 Magic Kingdom opens, followed by SeaWorld in 1973.

1990 Universal Studios opens.

1998 Animal Kingdom joins the theme parks at Walt Disney World® Resort.

1999 Universal Studios Islands of Adventure opens, followed by Discovery Cove in 2000.

THE SEMINOLES

In the Creek language, Seminole means "runaway" and these Native Americans got the name because they had fled the control of the European settlers farther north. The names of two of Orlando's three counties pay tribute to Florida's Native American past. Seminole County chose its name in 1913 when it split from Orange County. The third, Osceola, is named after the leader of the Seminoles during the 2nd Seminole Indian War.

THE BIG FREEZE

Winter had been progressing as normal when temperatures dropped to 24 degrees Fahrenheit (-6 degrees Celsius) on December 27, 1894. The whole citrus crop of the state withered on the branch. The weather returned to normal in January but worse was to come. On February 9, 1895 temperatures plummeted to 17 degrees Fahrenheit (-8 degrees Celsius) killing the trees that were the backbone of the industry. It took until 1912 for the citrus groves to recover.

Time to Shop

Below: Tommy Hilfiger store at the Premium Outlets mall
Below right: Festival Bay

Shopping is listed as the number one activity for international visitors to Orlando, even scoring above the world-beating attractions. And retail therapy also attracts domestic visitors to the city,

with 45 percent spending time spending cash. And here Orlando beats the competition again: It's one of the primary shopping cities in the country with 52 million sq ft (4.6 million sq m) of retail space and still growing.

The classic styling, good quality and exceptional value of American brand products makes shopping for everyday items such as clothing and household items particularly good value. For clothing, fashionable brands such as Tommy Hilfiger, Calvin Klein, DKNY, Levi and Timberland are the names to watch for.

Orlando is particularly famed for its "outlet" stores, where designer and mainstream brands sell end-of-line or seasonal items and lower-quality products at a discounted rate (savings of up to 70 percent on the American store price). Hundreds of thousands of square feet of retail space is devoted to low-cost shopping with stores conveniently gathered together in specialist shopping malls.

Though the city's predominant shopping environment for good-quality, mass-produced

SOMETHING OLD?

American collectibles form a small but interesting section of the Orlando shopping market. Genuine antiques date from the late 19th century, just before the coming of mass production and include pottery, glassware and original quilts and soft furnishings. Many portable items are hand-made and often bear the initials or name of the owner and the date they were made, making for a really personal souvenir.

consumer goods is the shopping mall, Orlando offers several farmers' markets and arts festivals throughout the year where you can buy one-of-a-kind arts-and-crafts items. The downtown

*Far left: family shopping trip
Left: lots of SpongeBob Squarepants toys at Universal Studios Islands of Adventure*

core, Winter Park and Celebration are the most favored locations.

No one should end a trip to Orlando without a souvenir of their favorite character, be it Spider-Man, Shamu®, Shrek or Spongebob Squarepants. All the parks have excellent on-site shopping where you can buy bona fide souvenirs from the glitzy to the kitsch, such as original and unique hand-drawn celluloid cartoon fiches to fridge magnets. Character embossed T-shirts and baseball caps are sold by the millions and are especially practical in the hot Florida climate.

Although there's something for every budget, prices are high. Quality is rigorously controlled and the elaborate and inventive store designs make shopping a real pleasure: Disney and Universal take as much care over store design as they do over their rides and shows.

Outside the park boundaries, other souvenir shops also cash in on the popularity of the theme parks but these will not be officially endorsed goods so beware quality differences.

SHOP THE WORLD

Epcot's World Showcase at Walt Disney World is a fantastic place to buy goods from around the world, from the exotic to the mundane, without needing to use your passport.
Choose from colorful cotton blankets and sombreros from Mexico; pure wool sweaters and toboggans from Norway; Steiff Teddy bears and ceramic beer steins from Germany; sheepskin bags and leather belts from Morocco; Limoge porcelain and Bordeaux wine from France; tea and tea-sets from the United Kingdom; jade and silk from China; Venetian glass from Italy and maple syrup from Canada.

19

Out and About

Below: SheiKra roller coaster at Busch Gardens
Right: Rocket Garden at the Kennedy Space Center

INFORMATION

Busch Gardens
✚ Off map
✉ Mailing address: 3605 East Bougainvillea Avenue, Tampa
☎ 813/887-5082 or 1 888/ 800-5447
🕐 Core hours 10–6, extended hours throughout the year
🍴 Numerous restaurants $$–$$$ and cafés $
🚌 Shuttle bus from Orlando is $10 per round-trip (free for holders of Flextickets). For details of schedules ☎ 1 800/221-1339
♿ Excellent
💰 Very expensive
How to get there: Take I-4 west then north on I75 following signs for Tampa. Exit at 265 on the I75 (University of South Florida) and take left off the exit ramp on Fowler Avenue. Turn left at Fowler's intersection with McKinley Drive and follow the road to the park entrance. Total distance 75 miles (120km); time 2 hours.

ORGANIZED SIGHTSEEING
ORLANDO TOURS

Orlando is not a destination that is conducive to organized tours. When so many of its attractions require at least half a day, or a full day for the major theme parks, the itineraries would be impossible. However, some theme parks offer tailormade tours as an extra package.

SeaWorld has a six-hour park tour with a guide and front-of-line access, guaranteed show seating and animal encounters. It also offers one-hour, behind-the-scenes tours for $16 (☎ 800/406-2244; **www.**seaworld.com).

Walt Disney World® Resort has several behind-the-scenes tours, but none have guided tours of the rides and shows. The full-day Backstage Magic explores behind the scenes at Epcot®, Disney-MGM Studios and Disney's Magic Kingdom® for $199. Others include the three-hour Gardens of the World at Epcot ($59) or the five-hour behind-the-scenes Keys to the Kingdom tour of Disney's Magic Kingdom ($58).

In downtown Orlando, the Regional History Center has guided tours on Saturday at 11am (free) where you can ask extra questions about Central Florida history. The Orlando Museum of Art will provide guided tours for 15 people or more ($7 per person).

EXCURSIONS
BUSCH GARDENS

Why include another theme park when, in that field, Orlando is the undisputed champion of the world? Busch Gardens combines several elements – animal attractions, rides, shows and

parades – to offer a balanced, one-day experience. The animal attractions, a series of intimate enclosures or vast environments that are part-ride, part-safari park, are first class. Natural landscapes have been meticulously re-created. Watch herds of giraffe, zebra and Thompson gazelle on the Serengeti Plain; visit the Edge of Africa with its hippos, baboons and meerkats, or ride Rhino Rally. The 2,700 animals make for close encounters by train, jeep ride or the Skyride, a four-man gondola that glides above the park.

Orlando has nothing like SheiKra, the USA's first "dive-coaster" with a 200ft (61m) ascent and a top speed of 70mph (112kph). It's a roller coaster aficionado's dream. And SheiKra is closely followed by all 7,000ft (650m) of Gwazi, the southeast's largest double coaster.

KENNEDY SPACE CENTER

The space race has captured public imagination since the 1960s, and the Kennedy Space Center has been at the heart of the action, launching the Apollo rockets that landed men on the moon and, more recently, the space shuttles. The visitor center is the place to immerse yourself in all things "zero-gravity."

There's lots of information about what happened to whom, when and how. Where else could you climb into a Space Shuttle without having to go through years of astronaut training? You can chat to a real astronaut or have your photograph taken with another in a space suit.

The serious parts of the tour take you to the NASA compound where launches are planned and executed. You'll visit the LC-39 Gantry, a 60ft (18m) tower with a 360-degree view of the complex and the shuttle launch bays, where you can experience a simulated take-off. Or visit the Apollo/Saturn V Center, which describes the heyday of American space exploration.

INFORMATION

Kennedy Space Center

✚ Off map

✉ State Road 405

☎ 321/452-2121 or 800/KSC-INFO, ticket line 321/449-4400

🕐 9am–dusk

🍴 Restaurant $$ and café $ facilities

♿ Excellent

💲 Very expensive

How to get there: Take Highway 50 east out of Orlando. At the first traffic light after passing the I-95, turn right on Highway 405 (also Columbia Drive). Follow Highway 405 to the Space Center. Total distance is 50 miles (80km); the journey takes about 80 minutes.

21

Walks

INFORMATION

Distance 4.5 miles (7km)
Time 3 hours, not including visits
Start point Peabody Hotel, International Drive
🔲 F7
🚍 Lynx route 8, 38 and 42; I-Ride
End point
🔲 G6
🚍 Lynx route 8, 38 and 42; I-Ride

Above: tee off at Pirate's Cove Adventure Golf
Below: inside Race Rock Café on International Drive

INTERNATIONAL DRIVE

With lots of opportunities to stop and extend your day, plus numerous tempting eateries, I-Drive makes a great walking route.

Make sure you are at the Peabody Hotel at 11am to see the "march of the ducks" then turn right out of the hotel to I-Drive. Stay on the right-hand side of the road as most of the attractions are here. At .3 mile (.5km) you'll come to Point*Orlando, the entertainment and shopping complex, followed by Wonderworks (➤ 35).

The official visitors' center is hard to see. Set in a small mall off the road after 1 mile (1.6km), it's a good place for advice and information. After passing Pirates Cove Adventure Golf and the Mercado, the quirky facade of Ripley's Believe It or Not comes into view.

Cross the major intersection at Sand Lake Road onto the main, neon-lit section of the route. Magical Midway offers karting and arcade rides before you turn the right-hand bend to Wet 'n' Wild (➤ 58).

Cross to the left-hand side of the road at the intersection of Universal Boulevard to view Skull Kingdom, a house of horrors, before passing Congo River Golf and the Sheraton Studio City Hotel. Cross Kirkman Road and Grand National Drive. Eventually the road sweeps left and you get your first views of the Belz malls (➤ 42) up ahead. You'll reach Belz Designer Outlets on the left and Festival Bay on the right. The well-known retail names might tempt you to start shopping immediately. If not, you've only got .2 mile (.3km) to reach Belz Outlet World and the end of your journey.

WINTER PARK

A compact little neighborhood but certainly the prettiest in Orlando, Winter Park has a variety of attractions.

Begin your journey at the Charles Hosmer Morse Museum of American Art and spend time enjoying the beautiful Tiffany glass collection. The gift shop is also a great place for purchasing interesting arty souvenirs.

Cross the street outside the front door (Park Avenue) and turn right, into the heart of some of the best shopping in the city. It's a great place for browsing and there are a couple of cafés for an early coffee stop.

When you reach Boulevard Avenue turn left and walk ahead for a block and a half until you reach Lake Osceola, the starting point for the scenic boat tour. An hour on the water will take you past some rather beautiful lakefront properties with waterfront views of Rollins College and Kraft Azalea Gardens.

After the cruise retrace your steps to Park Avenue and continue your journey south (turn left at the intersection). On the right-hand side of the street is Central Park. This open space is the venue for Winter Park's many festivals and summer concerts.

Above: street scene in Winter Park
Below: eating outside at a Winter Park café

Continue south past the Park Plaza Hotel and 310 Park South (you may want to peruse the menu for a late lunch or early dinner) until you reach Holt Avenue. Turn left here; the route leads you onto the campus of Rollins College. The college, founded in 1885, is famed for its Italianate styling and formal gardens.

Stay on Holt Avenue to visit Knowles Chapel, venue for the concerts of the Bach Festival, before moving on to the Cornell Museum of Fine Arts, which contains the oldest such collection in Florida with pieces as diverse as painting from the Rubens School and sculptures by Henry Moore.

INFORMATION

Distance 1 mile (1.5km)
Time 3.5 hours (more if you shop)
Start point
🚦 L1
🚌 Lynx routes 1, 9 and 23
End point
🚦 L1
🚌 Lynx routes 1, 9 and 13

Orlando by Night

Above and right: neon lights on CityWalk

THEME PARTY

The fun doesn't stop once the theme parks close, and as soon as you've seen the obligatory fireworks extravaganza you can start your evening entertainment. But that does not mean leaving Walt Disney World® Resort or Universal.

They've been quick to realize that the majority of visitors are adults who want evening entertainment as well as daytime fun. Both offer an excellent range of live music with local, national and international headline acts, clubs with resident and guest DJs, and comedy clubs. International Drive is also a hub of activities, with nightclubs and bars in the large hotel complexes around the convention center.

DOWNTOWN

If you want to mingle with Orlando's suburbanites, head for the downtown core. On sultry summer evenings Wall Street Plaza, a compact group of bars and restaurants that tumbles into the traffic-free street, has a buzzing atmosphere. Church Street's clubs are within walking distance, while a short taxi ride away you can stroll through Thornton Park with its chic eateries.

Orlando is the cultural core of central Florida and offers a well-rounded program of ballet, opera and concerts. The theaters at Loch Haven and the Bob Carr Center are the major venues, but Winter Park also hosts annual festivals.

Family fun also continues after dark. Dinner shows are a staple of Orlando's holiday scene and if you want to fight with pirates, joust with knights and cheer the hero these are all enjoyably well-choreographed events.

ORLANDO's
top 25 sights

The sights are shown on the maps on the inside front cover and inside back cover, numbered **1**–**25** across the region

© Disney

Disney's Animal Kingdom® Theme Park

HIGHLIGHTS

- DINOSAUR
- Festival of the Lion King show
- Flights of Wonder
- "It's Tough To Be a Bug!"® movie
- Kilimanjaro Safaris®
- Kali River Rapids®
- Maharajah Jungle Trek®
- Pangani Forest Exploration Trail®

INFORMATION

- ✚ A/B10
- ✉ P.O. Box 10000, Lake Buena Vista
- ☎ 407/824-4321
- 🕐 Core hours 9–5, open later in summer and holidays
- 🍴 Range of restaurants $$–$$$ and cafés $–$$
- 🚌 Lynx route 301
- ♿ Excellent
- 💲 Very expensive
- 🔗 Disney-MGM Studios (➤ 28), Downtown Disney® (➤ 33), Epcot® (➤ 29), Disney's Magic Kingdom® (➤ 27), Typhoon Lagoon (➤ 31)

Disney's film *The Lion King* sowed the seeds for this, the most recent addition to the Walt Disney World® Resort. Around the core of an excellent safari park, Disney has wrapped its inimitable razzmatazz of rides and shows.

Getting your bearings The park is divided into several areas, the major two being Asia and Africa with their live animal attractions. Disney's Animal Kingdom® Theme Park radiates from a central point, The Oasis, where you will find The Tree of Life, a 200ft (61m) baobab. Watch the energetic "It's Tough to be a Bug!"® 3-D movie here. Prehistoric creatures form the theme of DinoLand USA, and classic Disney makes an appearance in Camp Minnie-Mickey.

Live animals Disney's attention to detail is obvious in its flagship attraction Kilimanjaro Safaris®. Take a jeep tour on sun-bleached plains, complete with giraffes, antelope, hippos, rhino and ostriches. On foot in Africa you can enjoy the Pangani Forest Exploration Trail® where a family of gorillas is the star attraction.

Exotic creatures can also be found in the neighboring Asia "continent" in the fictitious land of Anandapur. Stroll among the ruins of an jungle temple at Maharajah Jungle Trek® to spot playful gibbons, Komodo dragons and giant bats while Asia's big cat has its own lair, the 5-acre (2ha) Tiger Range.

Artificial delights Disney works its magic with rides and shows to enhance your zoological odyssey. Flights of Wonder offers an entertaining insight into bird behavior, while Pocahontas and her friends introduce conservation to a young audience. The best rides are Asia's Kali River Rapids® and DinoLand's DINOSAUR.

© Disney

Disney's Magic Kingdom®

The original Orlando Disney park kick-started the city's meteoric rise to worldwide fame. Magic Kingdom® still captures the fairy-tale world of the Disney films: prepare to be charmed, beguiled and, probably, exhausted.

Getting your bearings Main Street USA, Disney's take on old town America, is as familiar to the world as Broadway or Oxford Street. It's the artery that leads to the heart of Magic Kingdom and from here to fabulous "lands," Adventureland, Frontierland®, Liberty Square, Fantasyland, Mickey's Toontown Fair and Tomorrowland® that radiate out forming the limbs of the park.

A character wonderland Cinderella Castle, at the entrance to Fantasyland, symbolizes Magic Kingdom®, creating a sense of wonder and awe that explains the reason for Disney's phenomenal success over the last 50 or so years. The "imagineers" have gone to enormous lengths to get every detail right; even the street lamps on Main Street USA cast shadows in the shape of Mickey Mouse ears when the sun shines.

Just for fun Magic Kingdom® is all about pure escapism, there's no educational motive. Each land has its collection of rides and shows, from roller coasters to 3-D animations. Many of the rides and shows link directly to Disney films so Dumbo, Peter Pan, Winnie the Pooh, Snow White and, more recently, Buzz Lightyear put in an appearance. The more challenging rides take you to places you wouldn't otherwise go: mountain summits, haunted houses or even into outer space. Mickey Mouse and pals make appearances throughout the park, but they have a permanent home in Mickey's Toontown Fair.

HIGHLIGHTS

- Cinderella Castle
- Main Street USA
- Pirates of the Caribbean
- Splash Mountain®
- Big Thunder Mountain Railroad
- The Haunted Mansion
- Peter Pan's Flight
- Mickey's PhilharMagic
- Space Mountain®
- The Timekeeper
- Buzz Lightyear's Space Ranger Spin

INFORMATION

- ✚ B8
- ✉ P.O. Box 10000, Lake Buena Vista
- ☎ 407/824-4321
- 🕐 Core hours daily 9–7, later depending on season
- 🍴 Numerous restaurants $$–$$$ and cafés $
- 🚌 Lynx route 302
- ♿ Excellent
- 💲 Very expensive
- ↔ Disney's Animal Kingdom® (➤ 26), Disney-MGM Studios (➤ 28), Downtown Disney® (➤ 33), Epcot® (➤ 29), Typhoon Lagoon (➤ 31)
- ❓ Special parades and events for major holidays

© Disney

Disney-MGM Studios

HIGHLIGHTS

- The Twilight Zone Tower of Terror™
- Rock 'n' Roller Coaster® Starring Aerosmith
- Star Tours – the ultimate Star Wars™ thrill ride
- Indiana Jones™ Epic Stunt Spectacular!
- Beauty and the Beast – Live on Stage
- Fantasmic!
- Voyage of the Little Mermaid
- Jim Henson's MuppetVision 3-D
- Playhouse Disney Live on Stage
- Disney-MGM Studios Backlot Tours

INFORMATION

- ➕ C10
- ✉ P.O. Box 10000, Lake Buena Vista
- ☎ 407/824-4321
- ◎ Core hours 9–7, extended hours depending on season
- 🍴 Range of restaurants $$–$$$ and cafés $
- 🚌 Lynx route 303
- ♿ Excellent
- 💲 Expensive
- ↔ Disney's Animal Kingdom® (▶ 26), Downtown Disney® (▶ 33), Epcot® (▶ 29), Typhoon Lagoon (▶ 31)
- ❓ Parades and celebrations throughout the year

Disney's homage to the glory days of MGM in Hollywood is an energetic romp through its cinematographic history, pausing for breath at several hit movies. Additionally, you can take a tour of working Disney studios.

Here we go The scene is set as you enter via Hollywood Boulevard rigged out in its 1930s heyday. In many ways The Great Movie Ride encapsulates the park. This high-speed train takes a whistle-stop tour around MGM classics from *Casablanca* to *Aliens*, giving each an extra thrill with the enhanced special effects. This is the park with Disney's most state-of-the-art electronic wizardry and it's not just films that get the treatment: TV shows and musicals also get their turn in the limelight.

Most of the rides at Disney-MGM are oriented more to adults and teenagers than young children. There isn't the invisible film of fairy dust that hangs in the air at Disney's Magic Kingdom®, but the park makes up for that with several entertaining live shows including film stunts explained in Indiana Jones™ Epic Stunt Spectacular! and the musical extravaganza Beauty and the Beast – Live on Stage.

Movie making? About half the park is accessed by a guided backlot tour, offering a comprehensive view of whatever happens to be being filmed at the time; whether it be a commercial or a full-length feature. Be aware, though that much of the Disney cartoon production now takes place in California, so you'll have little chance of seeing Mickey come to life on celluloid. You'll be able to enjoy the special effects water tank, prop room and genuine backlots, climaxing in the Catastrophe Canyon ride where you find yourself taking part in the action.

Epcot®

Epcot® was the project closest to Walt Disney's heart. The Experimental Prototype Community of Tomorrow was to be a high-tech global village that he hoped would act as a "think-tank" for the world's social problems.

Earth first Disney died before the concept was finalized and corporate Disney switched the emphasis from urban planning to Earth and technology. It delivers the fewest "thrills and spills" of Walt Disney World® Resort parks, but it's still lots of fun to explore our environment.

Future perfect The emblem of Epcot®, the much-photographed, golf ball-like Spaceship Earth, sits at the heart of Future World. Play with the latest technological gadgets at Innoventions: The Road to Tomorrow or dive deep into the physical world around you at The Living Seas, The Land or Universe of Energy. If you can't spend a day in Orlando without doing a ride, go to Mission: SPACE. This simulation puts you in one of NASA's missions, from the g-crunching launch to the weightlessness of orbit.

See the world Set around an artificial lagoon, World Showcase offers 11 geographical "zones" that span four continents. Each featured country or continent presents itself in microcosm, offering the chance to explore its finest national specialties, architecture or consumer products, as well as an ever-changing assortment of artisans, minstrels, native flora and food.

The USA sits at the halfway point of your 1.2 mile (2km) circular stroll, but since you'll find genuine America right outside the park, perhaps you'll want to spend more time visiting Japan with its Zen pagodas and rock gardens or France for the evocative film *Impressions of France*.

HIGHLIGHTS

- IllumiNations: Reflections of Earth
- Spaceship Earth
- The Living Seas
- Living with the Land
- "Honey, I Shrunk the Audience"
- Test Track
- Mission: SPACE
- Body Wars
- O Canada!

INFORMATION

- C9/10
- P.O. Box 10000, Lake Buena Vista
- 407/824-4321
- Daily Future World 9–9, World Showcase at 11–9
- Range of restaurants $$-$$$ and cafés $-$$
- Lynx routes 50, 56, 301 and 303
- Excellent
- Very expensive
- Disney's Animal Kingdom® (➤ 26), Disney-MGM Studios (➤ 28), Downtown Disney® (➤ 33), Disney's Magic Kingdom® (➤ 27), Typhoon Lagoon (➤ 31)
- Festivals throughout the year, including International Food Festival in October

29

Celebration

HIGHLIGHTS

- The slower tempo of the town
- The traditional architecture
- The Sunday farmers' market
- Strolling around the lake
- Browsing in the stores
- Carriage rides

INFORMATION

- Off map
- FL 34747
- Town Hall 407/566-1200, events hotline 407/566-2200
- 24 hours
- Range of restaurants $–$$$ and cafés $
- Very good
- Free, carriage rides expensive
- Old Town (► 32)
- Cultural and community events held throughout the year. Farmers' market on Sunday morning

Fun in the fountains

In the 1990s Disney picked up on a lost thread of Walt's dream and the Epcot experiment got a new lease of life, and extra realism, as this planned community, fusing traditional aesthetics and values with contemporary technology.

The foundations Criticized by some as "imagineering gone mad," Celebration has confounded its detractors by living up to its billing. The plans called for a new type of old-fashioned "hometown," the kind of town that feeds the imagination of American idealists. Celebration would include a lake with nature walks and cycle paths, wooden benches where you could while away an hour or two. Downtown shops would be intimate boutiques with sidewalks for browsing and ice-cream parlors from which to watch the world go by. The houses would look traditionally southeastern, with clapboard siding, a swing on the porch and a spick-and-span yard. Colonial Revival, Victorian and Craftsman styles created architectural variety, but overall homogeneity would be preserved by prescribed colors and finishes.

The finished product Ground was broken on a patch of native Florida landscape just southeast of the Walt Disney World® Resort in 1996. Today 10,000 Celebration residents benefit from modern amenities such as a hospital, high school, university campus, golf course and a 6,000sq ft (550sq m) fitness center.

The downtown core makes a relaxing place to spend a few hours. "Caribbeanesque" Market Street is certainly a welcoming place to combine a spot of shopping with a lazy lunch. Rest awhile by the lake before taking a carriage ride – or rent a cute electric car – for a tour around the impressive surrounding suburbs.

© Disney

Typhoon Lagoon

Orlando's only disadvantage as a family holiday destination was its lack of beaches. So Disney stepped in to provide what nature hadn't. Now you won't miss sand between your toes or the sound of waves lapping onshore.

Why Typhoon Lagoon? Typhoon Lagoon is styled as a tropical harbor in the aftermath of a storm. Flotsam and jetsam, including a full-size shrimp boat beached on high ground, is strewn around. All water parks have the same basic ingredients, but two elements set 56-acre (22ha) Typhoon Lagoon apart from the others: The amazing surf pool and the amount of shade the park offers on a sunny day.

Action or relaxation? For adrenaline addicts, Humunga Kowabunga is the most thrilling ride. Riders hit 30mph (45kph) on this fully covered 2,100ft (644m) waterslide, and navigate a five-story drop before seeing the light of day. At the opposite end of the scale, spend a lazy 45-minutes exploring the misty rain forest, caves and grottos of Castaway Creek. An impressive new ride, Crush'n'Gusher, opened in May 2005.

Surf's up The Surf Pool offers something the Atlantic and Pacific can't match; a constant fetch consisting of perfect 5ft (1.7m) breakers that arrive every 90 seconds brimming with white foam. Undercurrents or swells never sway the wave machine and there are no rocks or sharks to spoil your day whether you ace or bail. For perfect technique, you can take surfing lessons (3 mornings, 6.30am–9am).

Shark Reef Disney ensures that you're not snorkeling with any dangerous denizens of the deep; your swim companions are small, safe sharks.

HIGHLIGHTS

- Shark Reef
- Castaway Creek
- Humunga Kowabunga
- Surf Pool

INFORMATION

- ✚ D10
- ✉ P.O. Box 10000, Lake Buena Vista
- ☎ 407/560-4141
- 🕐 Core hours 10–6, extended hours depending on season
- 🍴 Café $
- 🚌 Lynx routes 301, 302 and 303
- ♿ Excellent
- 💲 Very expensive
- ↔ Disney's Animal Kingdom® (➤ 26), Disney-MGM Studios (➤ 28), Downtown Disney® (➤ 33), Epcot® (➤ 29) Disney's Magic Kingdom® (➤ 27)

Old Town

Head back to 1950s USA, where Rock 'n' Roll was a new craze and teenagers had just been invented. Frothy coffee was the drink of choice, blue jeans were tight and leather jackets black.

HIGHLIGHTS

- Classic car parades
- Specialty shopping
- Old-fashioned fun fair
- Live music
- Hometown main street ambience

INFORMATION

- ✚ D11
- ✉ 5770 West US Highway 192
- ☎ 407/396-4888 or 800/843-4202
- 🕐 Daily, shops 10am–11pm, amusements noon–11
- 🍴 Range of restaurants $$ and cafés $
- 🚌 Lynx routes 55 and 56
- ♿ Very good
- 💵 Free, rides cheap
- ↔ Celebration (▶ 30)
- ❓ Program of vehicular special events throughout the year

Let's head into town Old Town is yet another Orlando "illusion." It re-creates that weekend across American when the fair rolled into town and everyone from Grandma to the kids turned out to enjoy the fun. Bumper cars and a merry-go-round hark back to that era, while rides are brought up to date with the high-energy Wave Swinger and Slingshot, a kind of reverse bungee jump that offers a view of Kissimmee from 365ft (111m) (if you have the courage to open your eyes at the time). Along Old Town Main Street you'll find a Haunted House and Hollywood Wax Museum along with "test your strength" machines. Seventy-five specialty shops sell "one of a kind" merchandise from joke nametags and irreverent T-shirts to Native American crafts and healing crystals. There's live music every night on the Old Town stage.

"Cruise Nite" Like any '50s town, it comes alive at weekends with a chance for mods, rockers, Sharks and Jets to show off their "wheels." Saturday night is classic night with 300 pre-1970s automobiles, antiques and hot rods (parade starts at 8.30pm; cars assemble from 1pm). Friday night moves forward in time with cars from 1973 to 1987, including souped-up Corvettes and supercharged Mustangs (parade at 9pm with cars assembling from 5pm). There's a chance to chat with owners and get a few tips on maintenance – but it would be hard to match the attention to detail and love that they lavish on their vehicles.

Downtown Disney®

What to do after the parks close? Visit Disney's lakeside shopping, dining and entertainment complex. Three distinct spheres make up the whole, each with its own character and purpose.

Marketplace The Marketplace is Disney's "shopping central" if you don't hit the parks themselves (you don't need a park ticket to shop here). It brings together 20 shops crammed with "mouse-approved" merchandise, interspersed with eateries. If you are a Disney fan you'll find an abundance of choice whatever your budget.

Pleasure Island A 6-acre (2.5ha) entertainment complex, Pleasure Island is set off the shore of Village Lake and is accessible by three bridges (allowing Disney to control entry). It's a great mix of nightclubs, comedy theaters and live music venues fostering a mixture of musical styles from rock, jazz and disco to Latin and techno. For a one-off payment you can tour all the clubs, enjoying live comedy performances before taking a turn on the dance floor. Pleasure Island achieves an effective transition from a family to an adult crowd as evening turns to night. After 9pm, it's adult Disney at its best.

West Side Disney has gone all out to ensure quality at this 70-acre (28ha) shopping and entertainment complex. Retail provision is anchored by a huge Virgin Megastore, and augmented by a host of high-quality outlets such as Hoypoloi – selling unique arts and crafts from across the USA.

It is also home to the unique Cirque du Soleil® show La Nouba™, and the House of Blues® with excellent live music. Enjoy the innovative menu at Wolfgang Puck® or eat Cuban at Bongo's Cuban Café®.

INFORMATION

- ✚ D/E9
- ✉ Lake Buena Vista Drive
- ☎ 407/396-4888
- 🕐 Daily 10am–11pm (bars and clubs until 2am)
- 🍽 Several restaurants $$ and fast-food eateries $
- 🚌 Lynx routes 300, 301, 302, 303 and 304
- ♿ Excellent
- 🎟 Free; access to Pleasure Island moderate
- ↔ Disney's Animal Kingdom® (➤ 26), Disney-MGM Studios (➤ 28), Epcot® (➤ 29), Disney's Magic Kingdom® (➤ 27), Typhoon Lagoon (➤ 31)

International Drive

HIGHLIGHTS

- Ripley's Believe It or Not!
- Wet 'n' Wild
- Titanic – The Exhibition
- Skull Kingdom
- The Peabody Ducks

INFORMATION

- South to north: F8, G8, F7, G6
- 24 hours
- Range of restaurants $–$$$ and cafés $
- Lynx routes 8, 38 and 42; I-Ride
- Very good
- Free
- Belz (➤ 42), Discovery Cove (➤ 40), SeaWorld (➤ 39), Wonderworks (➤ 35)

Ripley's Believe It or Not!
- 8201 International Drive
- 407/363-4418
- Daily 9am–1am
- Very good
- Moderate

Titanic – The Exhibition
- 8445 International Drive
- 407/248-1166
- Daily 10–10
- Very good
- Moderate

Wet 'n' Wild
- 6200 International Drive
- 407/351-1800
- Core hours 10–5
- Very good
- Very expensive

Also known as I-Drive, this bustling, 5-mile (3km) strip of hotels and restaurants was Orlando's reaction to the tourism boom of the 1970s. Smaller, independent tourist attractions and shops entertain visitors.

New challenges The area has had a fight on its hands since the late 1990s. Both Disney and Universal developed their own resort hotels and entertainment complexes, drawing visitors away. However, I-Drive has evolved to keep abreast of changing tastes and now boasts 100 hotels, 150 themed restaurants, 485 shops and 3 stadium-style cinemas.

What to do I-Drive offers lots of family fun and enough attractions to fill a few days. Several "adventure golf" courses and a couple of karting arcades set the scene. Wet 'n' Wild, the major water park outside Disney, has been responsible for some cutting-edge innovations over the past few years. The styling isn't quite on Disney's level but the thrills are good. At Ripley's Believe It or Not! you can explore a vast collection of strange and wondrous objects ranging from the creepy (shrunken heads) to the unbelievable (a three-quarter-scale 1907 Rolls Royce made of matchsticks). Titanic – The Exhibition is no less impressive with exact re-creations of rooms aboard, costumes from the film and poignant items salvaged from the doomed ship. For shopping on I-Drive, head north for Belz and Festival Bay, and south to the bargains of Orlando Premium Outlet Mall. Along the way, both Mercado and Pointe*Orlando offer yet more retail therapy.

I-Drive often experiences traffic gridlock, so relieve the strain a little and use I-Ride, the bus service that links all I-Drive's attractions.

Wonderworks

A secret science lab was torn from its site by a tornado and landed upside down on International Drive. The hundreds of experiments inside are still in perfect working condition, waiting for you – the scientists – to try them out.

Welcome in The gateway into Wonderworks sets the scene for the rest of the crazy, mind-boggling attraction. An inversion tunnel turns what should be a straightforward 10ft (3m) walk into a fight between mind and body. You know that it's just a matter of putting one foot in front of the other, but your eyes fool your mind into thinking you are falling and you end up clinging to the side rail. No matter what you tell your body, it won't stand tall.

A walk down memory lane Here you'll find low-tech games such as the fun fair favorites of the 1960s and '70s, wire and loop games, the Wonderwall of pins against which you can make shapes with your body, and a hall of mirrors. For something a little different try lying on a bed of nails. Or try unraveling the mind-bending drawings of M.C. Escher.

High-tech hardware Wonderworks finds lots of fun ways to showcase technology. The computerized ageing machines seem more popular with children than adults (the older you get, the less you want to know how you'll look in 20 years) but the elastic morphing, which has been used to great effect in films like *The Mask*, captures the imagination of all ages. The 3-D 360-degree freedom of movement of the Virtual Reality machine is an out-of-body experience. Or you can play with sound: morph your voice, play the giant piano like Tom Hanks in *Big*, or create a symphony in lights with Terpsichore.

HIGHLIGHTS

● Virtual Reality machine
● Escher designs
● Elastic morphing machine
● Bed of nails
● Hurricane experience
● Voice morphing

INFORMATION

✚ F7
✉ Pointe*Orlando, 9067 International Drive, Exit 74A
☎ 407/352-0411
◷ Daily 9am–midnight
🍴 Café $
🚌 Lynx routes 8, 38 and 42; I-Ride
♿ Very good
💲 Moderate (lazer tag extra – cheap)
🔗 Belz (► 42), Discovery Cove (► 40), International Drive (► 34), SeaWorld (► 39)

Universal Studios Florida™

Universal's arrival in Orlando gave adults something to cheer about. At last a park that didn't "sugar coat" the theme park experience and that didn't set an upper limit on exhilaration.

Basic principles Universal's vast catalog of box-office hits was fertile ground for ride "imagineers" and the company set out to bring the thrills of its films to the visitor experience. It developed the technological gadgetry that was revolutionizing Hollywood to use in a theme park: There isn't one mainstream outdoor coaster ride here. The buzz at Universal comes from robotics, pyrotechnics and 3-D visuals.

The experience Back To The Future The Ride® kick-started the whole process and despite the vintage status of the original movies, the ride is as popular and cutting edge as ever. Universal moved to the next level with Terminator 2®: 3-D and upped the ante again with MEN IN BLACK™ – Alien Attack™ before launching its latest offering – Revenge of the Mummy™.

But the kids aren't totally left wanting. Scooby Doo and Shaggy have fans from age 7 to 70 and legions of young, daytime fans guaranteed that Nickelodeon Studios® would be a runaway success when the park launched. Shrek is the box office's most bankable current cartoon star and his latest attraction is an exciting 4-D experience (see panel page 55).

Universal is still a working film studios and you can wander through the backlots to watch the latest scenes in progress. There's usually more going on here than at the studios at Disney-MGM.

Universal Studios Islands of Adventure™

Islands of Adventure, Universal's second park, has true all-round appeal. Less adult-oriented than Univeral Studios Florida, it has excellent rides and attractions for all ages.

The idea For many of these rides, Universal went back to basics. Sheer speed, stomach-turning drops and lots of water are the simple tools used to create sheer exhilaration, wrapped in convincing fantasy styling. The park consists of several "islands," most of which take a Universal or Nickelodeon theme.

Take the tour Marvel Super Hero Island® has two of the parks big-hitting attractions, The Amazing Adventures of Spider-Man® with its astonishing special effects and Incredible Hulk Coaster®, which is a speed merchant's dream.

Remember the fun that Popeye had on the high seas? You can immerse yourself in his watery world at Toon Lagoon. At the far reaches of the park, enter the primeval world of Jurassic Park, where designers have introduced the park's only "educational" element, the Discovery Center filled with genuine bones and skeletons. But even here the fun factor outweighs everything else. Jurassic Park River Adventures® sends you hurtling through the ancient world, with a few surprises on the way.

Incredible Hulk Coaster® has a serious rival for best roller coaster in Dueling Dragons® at The Lost Continent. This Arabian Nights-themed area hosts Islands of Adventure's major show, The Eighth Voyage of Sinbad.

Last but not least is Seuss Landing®. For millions of "Cat in the Hat" fans, it's a chance to meet their hero, listen to their favorite rhyming couplet and even eat "green eggs and ham" at the eponymous café.

HIGHLIGHTS

● Seuss Landing®
● Dueling Dragons®
● Poseidon's Fury®
● Jurassic Park River Adventures®
● Dudley Do-Right's Ripsaw Falls®
● The Amazing Adventures of Spider-Man®
● Incredible Hulk Coaster®

INFORMATION

✚ F6
✉ 1000 Universal Plaza
☎ 407/363-8000
🕐 Core hours 9–7, extended hours by season
🍴 Range of restaurants $$–$$$ and cafés $–$$
🚌 Lynx routes 21, 37 and 40
♿ Very good
💲 Very expensive
🔁 CityWalk (► 38), Universal Studios Florida™ (► 36)
❓ Other relevant information (including tours, lectures and special events)

Universal CityWalk®

Dance the night away at the Shamrock 'n' Roll extravaganza on St. Patrick's Day, lubricated by green beer. CityWalk doesn't need an excuse for a party, but if there is one, it pulls out all the stops.

The concept CityWalk is all about great food, classic cocktails and the chance to strut your stuff on the dance floor. Universal trawled the playgrounds of North America and the Caribbean for inspiration for its self-contained entertainment complex, drawing on the most happening themes and venues. With its cafés, restaurants and combined eateries and clubs, it's an easy place to let the late afternoon post-park relaxation slip into an evening meal followed by a night on the town. It's all in one place.

The itinerary The evening always kicks off with live music or some kind of live performance at CityWalk Stage. You can sip a mint julep in the Latin Quarter, stroll to The Big Easy, enjoy a hurricane in Pat O'Brien's, then spend a couple of hours in Nassau savoring a margarita at Margaritaville before "jetting" off to Jamaica for a rum at Bob Marley – A Tribute to Freedom™. Each venue brings a change of atmosphere and a change of musical style, and the all-inclusive ticket price means you don't need to pay at every door. If this itinerary sounds like a sure way to pick up a hangover, you're probably right, and it's wise to pace yourself.

CityWalk also allows you to combine activities for a set price. Take in an early movie at the multiplex cinema, then hit the clubs, or have a meal at one of the restaurants, then head to the dance floor. You can enjoy live concerts throughout the year on the open-air stage or at Hard Rock Live auditorium. For the current calendar of events visit **www.citywalkorlando.com**

SeaWorld

Bringing the ocean's life to Orlando, SeaWorld is a combination of aquatic zoo, animal encounters and shows. It's also a research and rescue facility for rare or sick marine creatures.

Let's explore The park is divided into a number of different sectors with water temperatures ranging from freezing to tropical to accommodate their inhabitants.

Dolphin Cove is one of the most popular areas of the park. The dolphins playfully skirt the edges of the environment so that everyone gets a chance to stroke their flanks. It gets pretty crowded with people at the posted feeding times, when the keepers give an entertaining and educational talk. Close by, there's a dolphin nursery where you can catch up with SeaWorld's latest arrivals.

Manatees are one of the most endangered of Florida's native creatures and these huge salad eaters – also known as "sea cows" – have their own quiet corner to live in. The manatee rescue program has so far saved over 270 animals. Each is vital for the future survival of this unusual species of mammal.

In contrast to the warm tropical waters of the manatee enclosure, Wild Arctic is an excellent, though frosty, encounter with polar bears, one of the far north's most awe-inspiring mammals.

Other attractions Shamu the Killer Whale is the emblem of the park and he's the leading star in his own show, but other park shows are equally entertaining, including Clyde and Seamore Take Pirate Island, starring a hilarious sea lion and otter double act.

SeaWorld has also bowed to pressure and built two rides, the watery Journey to Atlantis and Kraken, the best roller coaster in the city.

HIGHLIGHTS

- The Shamu® Show
- Dolphin Cove
- Penguin Encounter
- Wild Arctic
- Kraken
- Shark Encounter
- Clyde and Seamore Take Pirate Island

INFORMATION

- ➕ F/G8
- ✉ 700 SeaWorld Drive
- ☎ 407/351-3600
- 🕐 Core hours 9–7, later in summer
- 🍽 Restaurants $$ and several cafés $–$$
- 🚌 Lynx routes 8, 43 and 50; I-Ride
- ♿ Excellent
- 💲 Very expensive
- ↔ Discovery Cove (➤ 40), International Drive (➤ 34), Wonderworks (➤ 35)
- ❓ Seasonal special events

39

Discovery Cove

Orlando's newest major attraction, and sibling of SeaWorld, Discovery Cove was opened in 2000 after research showed that visitors were looking for a more intimate, personal vacation experience.

HIGHLIGHTS

- Dolphin Lagoon
- Coral Reef
- Ray Lagoon
- Tropical River
- Aviary
- Beaches

INFORMATION

- ✚ F/G8
- ✉ 6000 Discovery Cove Way
- ☎ 407/363-3380
- ⏰ Daily 8–5.30. Twilight sessions 3pm–9pm
- 🍽 Restaurant and café (included in the ticket price)
- 🚌 Lynx routes 8 and 50; I-Ride
- ♿ Excellent
- 💲 Very expensive (all inclusive of meals, snacks and equipment and pass to SeaWorld)
- ↔ SeaWorld (► 39), International Drive (► 34), Wonderworks (► 35)

The perfect hideaway The park is designed around a tropical lagoon with white-sand beaches with swaying palms and hammocks. It feels like a tropical resort and, because you share this hideaway with a maximum of 999 other people, there are no crowds, no queues – just a chance to chill out.

Let's make a new friend Discovery Cove's unique attraction is the Dolphin Encounter, a personal interaction with one of nature's most loveable creatures. Small groups of eight or so people, guided by a trainer, head into the dolphin pool for a well-orchestrated interaction during which you can touch, swim or play ball with one of these intelligent mammals.

Exploring Discovery Cove While you wait for your encounter – the undoubted highlight of your day – you can enjoy the other environments around the park. Swim and snorkel among shoals of tropical fish at the Coral Reef or get up close and personal with rays at Ray Lagoon. The Tropical River offers the chance to drift along in warmer waters and relax beneath the cascades, while the Aviary has over 250 exotic birds, many of which will feed from your hand.

More like a party During summer evenings Discovery Cove offers the Twilight Discovery program for up to a maximum of 100 guests so you feel like you're at a private party.

Wekiwa Springs State Park

Wekiwa (the Creek Native word for "spring") is a 7,800-acre (3,156ha) safe haven for a host of indigenous wildlife. The landscape has changed little in millennia and native Timucuan people once thrived in its pristine scenery.

Environment More than 700 freshwater springs issue from the Florida substrate and these are invaluable in maintaining the natural wetland environment. The main spring here spews out 43 million gallons (195 million liters) of water per day that flow north down the Wekiva River to meet the St. John's River before making their way out to the Atlantic at Jacksonville.

Within the park, 19 separate habitats, ranging from freshwater swamps at the lower levels up through pine flatwoods and hammock forests to dry sandy ridges, offer more diversity than any other park in the state and support a wealth of wildlife. Seventy-three plant species provide protection to important bird populations, including 34 species of warbler. Common animal species include white-tailed deer, raccoons, armadillo, opossum and turtles, while rarer animals for whom Wekiwa acts as a lifeline include the southern black bear, bobcat, bald eagle, gray fox and florida mouse, a rodent found only in this state.

Access A boardwalk skirts the southern stretches of wetland, hiking trails of varying lengths lead into the higher cypress and oak woodland, and in summer you can rent horses for riding. But perhaps the most exciting way to enjoy the park is by canoe. From the rental dock close to the spring you can head out into the Wekiwa River bordered by a vast natural swampland where you can imagine yourself in the Florida of yesteryear.

FLORIDA BEAR FACTS

- Black bears are the only bears native to Florida.
- Bear numbers have grown from 10 in 1980 to more than 1,100 in 2000.
- The largest bear recorded in Florida was a male of 624 pounds (283kg).
- Bears are omnivores, eating both vegetable matter and meat.
- About 80 percent of a Florida bear's diet is plants, nuts and berries.
- Bears are good climbers.
- Florida black bears do not hibernate.
- In Florida bear cubs are born in late January or early February.
- It is illegal to feed bears.

INFORMATION

➕ Off map

✉ 1800 Wekiwa Circle, Apopka (I-4 east to Exit 94, left to Wekiwa Springs Road, turn right, drive 4 miles (6km) to park entrance on right)

☎ 407/884-2008

🕐 Daily 8am–sunset

♿ Few

💷 Per vehicle: cheap

❓ Only 300 vehicles are allowed into the park, so arrive early on holidays and summer weekends. Guided talks and open days during the summer

Belz

HIGHLIGHTS

- Bargain official theme park merchandise
- Goods sold at up to 70 percent discount on the US retail price
- Quality brand names

INFORMATION

- G5/6
- 5401 West Oak Ridge Road
- 407/354-0126
- Daily Mon–Sat 10–9, Sun 11–6
- Cafés $
- Lynx routes 8, 38 and 42; I-Ride
- Excellent
- Free
- International Drive (► 34), Wonderworks (► 35)

Belz is the mall that brought factory outlet shopping to central Orlando. There are more elegant temples to retailing in the city, but Belz is still the place for seasoned bargain hunters.

Why Orlando? Shopping is big business in Orlando. Almost 50 million visitors a year arrive toting credit cards on the lookout for a souvenir or a gift or two. And a fast-growing population fueled by retirees from the colder north, overseas second homeowners, and a buoyant jobs market means people want to spend and they have the disposable income to do it.

The facts Belz statistics make pretty impressive reading: almost 1 million sq ft (93,000sq m) of shopping is divided into two sections. The original Factory Outlet store has 700,000sq ft (65,000sq m) of enclosed shopping while the more upscale Designer Outlet currently stands at 200,000sq ft (18,000sq m). Many of America's famous retail names are here, including Calvin Klein, Liz Claiborne, Nike, Nine West, Oshkosh B'gosh, Timberland and Van Heusen. The theme parks have seen the advantage of leasing space – you'll find end-of-line Disney and Universal bargains, as well as current (full-price) souvenirs.

Shop until you drop While clothing stores predominate, Belz also attracts high-calibre shops in a number of retail sectors and it's almost possible to furnish a whole house from top to bottom in one visit. Excellent international brands, such as Waterford for blown lead crystal, offer goods that are not easy to find elsewhere in the US, especially at these prices.

Gatorland

The toothiest grins in Orlando are at Gatorland. This is the best place to get close to Florida's most enigmatic creature, the American alligator, a species unchanged for millions of years.

Denizens of the swamps Younger children aren't always convinced that these huge monsters are real, but don't be deceived by the statue-like demeanor of the hundreds of basking adult alligators on show here and climb over the fences. This species can move at lightning speed over short distances.

Alligators and crocodiles are cold-blooded species and need heat to raise their body temperature to get active, so the huge adults – up to 15ft (4.5m) in length – spend much of their time inert and soaking up the sun. The only time there's any real movement is at show time, when the hunks of meat dangled temptingly a few feet above those leathery snouts cause a frenzy of snapping jaws.

Younger, and decidedly more cute, alligators and hatchlings bask in smaller enclosures, often piled one atop another to reach the hottest spot.

Behind the pens, a verdant tropical waterhole plays host to a number of breeding pairs, observable from a boardwalk. Always open to an opportunity (read, eager for free food), the waterhole has a complicated ecology with populations of egrets, Everglades herons, turtles and frogs, but they have to be careful not to end up as breakfast!

Gatorland also has a small collection of other exotic animals and hosts several "hands-on" shows every day where you can stroke a snake or pet a parrot. You can take a tour around the outer enclosure on a miniature train or explore the swamp trail on foot.

DID YOU KNOW?

- The name alligator comes from the Spanish "el lagarto" or "the lizard."
- In the 1960s, the American alligator was an endangered species.
- Today there are hundreds of thousands of wild 'gators in Florida alone.
- They lose their appetites when the temperature drops below 27°C (80°F) and can go for months without food.
- Alligators build elaborate nests and lay eggs.
- The temperature of the egg in the nest decides the sex of a baby alligator.

INFORMATION

- ✚ J10
- ✉ 14501 South Orange Blossom Trail
- ☎ 407/855-5496
- 🕐 Daily 9–5
- 🍴 Café $
- 🚌 Lynx route 4
- ♿ Good
- 💰 Moderate

Orange County Regional History Center

Even cities as modern and forward-looking as Orlando have a fascinating history. The Regional History Center pulls together the threads of the Central Florida story.

All rise... Set in the old Orange County Courthouse, erected in 1927 at the heart of downtown, Orlando's History Center opened in 2000 after a $35m refurbishment. There's a wealth of information here and it has been carefully and beautifully dramatized with depictions of the major lifestyles from throughout Florida's long history.

Follow the timeline The first stop on the tour is Orientation Theater. Relax in a rocker on a Florida back porch, while surrounded by the sights and sounds of old and new Central Florida, before you immerse yourself in Timucuan culture. These fascinating people welcomed the Spanish when they ventured inland in the 16th century, but within a few decades they were wiped out by diseases, introduced to the area by ships from Europe, to which they had no immunity.

Fast forward to the early 1800s and you can explore a Seminole settlement and Cracker home. These two peoples lived side-by-side. They were anti-establishment, proud and highly adapted to their environment. Around the campfire you'll learn how both got their names before you head into the late 1800s and find yourself surrounded by the citrus groves that are still a mainstay of the Florida economy.

The museum provides a fascinating background on Orlando's meteoric rise at the very end of 20th century, with photographs showing the construction of Magic Kingdom and the development of the modern city.

Orlando Science Center

The aim of the Orlando Science Center is to help all age groups understand complicated theories. It's "hands-on" learning, with exhibits designed with the help of theme park "imagineers."

Let's make science fun Many of the exhibits are linked to science curricula at various grades, so you can assess suitability for each age group. Kid's Town is perfect for little pre-schoolers as the world is shrunk to their own size. BodyZone is another bright, fun area that explores how we see, hear, move or digest food. It also promotes healthy eating and lifestyle choices. You can then move on to Measure Me and explore how food becomes energy, strength and agility.

Moving on Other areas explore the scientific principles that govern our physical world. Exhibits here are more suited to older children, and adults. At Physics Park, investigate practical applications of physics including the rules that influence building design. The Power Station delves into the world of electricity – how it's generated and how it gets to your home. Then focus on Light Power; how lasers, optics, prisms, mirrors and the electromagnetic spectrum affect our daily lives. The Dr. Phillips CineDome features the world's largest Iwerks domed screen, where the films are projected all around the audience for maximum sensory overload.

Serious science The Tech Works is a real laboratory fitted out with cutting-edge technology. You'll find the region's only public access electron microscope here, while Florida's largest public access refractor telescope is located at the Digistar Planetarium, allowing amateur astronomers the chance to observe stars, moons and planets.

HIGHLIGHTS

- The Dr. Phillips CineDome
- BodyZone
- Kid's Town
- Digistar Planetarium
- Light Power
- The Cosmic Tourist

INFORMATION

- K2
- 777 East Princeton Street
- 407/514-2000
- Tue–Thu 9–5; Fri–Sat 9–9; Sun noon–5. Closed Mon except school holidays when 9–5
- Café $
- Lynx routes 1, 9 and 39
- Excellent
- Orlando Museum of Art (➤ 46), Harry P. Leu Gardens (➤ 47), Winter Park (➤ 48)
- Moderate. After 6pm Fri–Sat cheap
- Guest lectures. Monthly schedule of events

45

Orlando Museum of Art

HIGHLIGHTS

- Avian Pendant: gold jewelry from Costa Rica dating from AD1000–1500
- Carved Greenstone Yoke: used during ancient ball games in Mexico (AD300–900)
- The Sun Vow: a bronze by Hermon Atkins MacNeil (c1901)
- Male Effigy Jar from the Recuay peoples of central Peru (AD100–300)

INFORMATION

- K2
- 2416 North Mills Avenue, I-4 to Exit 85, head east
- 407/896-4231
- Tue–Fri 10–4, Sat–Sun noon–4; closed Mon
- Lynx route 39
- Excellent
- Cheap
- Orlando Science Center (➤ 45), Harry P. Leu Gardens (➤ 47), Winter Park (➤ 48)
- Gallery tours and lectures

Portrait vessel from Peru (AD250–500)

The Orlando Museum of Art's reputation is founded on its American tribal artifacts. It also exhibits varied post-Independence art and a fascinating collection of native African crafts.

American Art This eclectic collection covers the full range of American history and comprises paintings, prints, drawings, photos and sculpture. Notable artists include John Singer Sargent, Georgia O'Keeffe, one of the 20th century's most influential women artists, and Ansel Adams, founding father of landscape photography. The smaller Contemporary American Graphics Collection displays works by Andy Warhol and Jasper Johns, two of the founders of the "Pop Art" movement.

Ancient American Art Collection The Art of the Ancient Americas Collection is now the best in the southern US, boosted by impressive donations over the last couple of years by Dr. Solomon D. Klotz (deceased) and Harriet Klotz. Over 30 different cultural groups are represented from throughout North, South and Central America and artifacts range in date from 2000BC to 1521. The collection is particularly strong in artifacts of the Pueblo cultures of the American Southwest, the Anasazi of the southern Colorado Plateau, and their close relatives, the Mogollon of the high Chihuahuan Desert.

African Art Collection This is an excellent collection of ceremonial and everyday artifacts from various parts of Africa, including intricate Zulu and Xhosa beadwork and basketware. The most interesting objects belong to the Dogon and their fascinating funerary and death rituals, which incorporate ritual masked dances to guide the spirit of the dead to its final resting place.

Harry P. Leu Gardens

The Leu estate is a tribute to Orlando-born Harry P. Leu who, after purchasing this 1850s estate, amassed a superb collection of plants to start one of America's finest tropical gardens.

The gardens The Leu estate has several botanical highlights within its 50-acre (20ha) extent. It is home to one of the largest camellia collections on the east coast, with more than 2,000 species (best viewed between October and March) and the largest formal rose garden in Florida, containing nearly 250 varieties (a riot of color throughout the year). You can also explore the largest banana collection in the USA, a butterfly garden with native plants to attract lepidoptera large and small, a white garden and a fragrant herb garden. A maze of paths meanders among these different natural environments, and the whole collection sits under a canopy of mature native oaks.

History The Leu house itself is worthy of exploration. Overlooking a lakeshore, the central part of the mansion was erected in 1858 by Angeline and David Mizell, who farmed cotton where the gardens now stand. Mizell was also an Orange County sheriff; he was shot dead in 1870 during a feud between the Mizell and Barber families. The house reached its present size during the first decades of the 20th century, under the ownership of the Pell and Woodward families.

Businessman Harry P. Leu bought the property in 1936 and immediately began to work on plans to turn the garden into a tropical paradise. The Leus traveled extensively, bringing back plants, tubers and seeds for their growing collection. The house has been painstakingly restored to its turn-of-the-19th-century style and is listed in the National Register of Historic Places.

HIGHLIGHTS

- The Camellia Garden
- The Rose Garden
- The White Garden
- The Herb Garden
- The lakeshore views
- Leu Mansion
- The xerophyte (plants that need little water) garden
- The cycads (ancient palms abundant during the Jurassic period) collection

INFORMATION

- 🧭 K2
- ✉ 1920 N. Forest Avenue
- ☎ 407/246-2620
- 🕐 Daily 9–5, longer hours in summer
- 🍴 Café $
- 🚌 Lynx routes 2 and 13
- ♿ Very good
- 💷 Cheap
- 🔗 Orlando Science Center (➤ 45), Orlando Museum of Art (➤ 46), Winter Park (➤ 48)
- ❓ Lectures, special seasonal displays throughout the year

47

Winter Park

HIGHLIGHTS

- Kraft Azalea Gardens
- Charles Hosmer Morse Museum of American Art
- Museum of Fine Arts
- Scenic boat tour

INFORMATION

- ➕ L1
- ☎ Events: 407/623-3363
- 🍽 Cafés, restaurants $–$$$
- 🚌 Lynx routes 1, 9 and 23
- 🚉 Amtrak station
- 🎫 Free
- ↔ Orlando Science Center (➤ 45), Harry P. Leu Gardens (➤ 47)
- ❓ Sat farmers' market

The Albin Polasek Museum
- ✉ 633 Osceola Avenue
- ☎ 407/647-6294
- 🕐 Sep–Jun, Thu–Sat 10–4, Sun 1–4

Scenic Boat Tour
- ✉ 312 East Morse Boulevard
- ☎ 407/644-4056
- 🕐 Daily 10–4

Charles Hosmer Morse Museum of American Art
- ✉ 445 North Park Avenue
- ☎ 407/645-5311
- 🕐 Tue–Thu, Sat 9.30–4; Sep–May, Fri 9.30–8; Jun–Aug, Fri 9.30–4, Sun 1–4

Cornell Fine Arts Museum
- ✉ 1000 Holt Avenue
- ✉ 407/646-2526
- 🕐 Tue–Fri 10–5, Sat–Sun 1–5

The most urbane of Orlando's suburbs, Winter Park makes a refreshing departure from the theme parks, especially for those in search of some culture.

Foundations Winter Park was founded by David Mizell (➤ 47) in 1858 and in 1881 businessmen Loring Chase and Oliver Chapman bought 600 acres (242ha). The arrival of the railroad in 1882 sealed the success of the settlement. Rollins College, established in 1885, quickly became an academic center of excellence. Early in the 20th century, when northerners would come to enjoy the temperate winters, the largest hotel in Florida was built here. Today, Winter Park is a desirable address, with great shopping on the main boulevard, Park Avenue.

Museums The Charles Hosmer Morse Museum of American Art houses one of the most comprehensive collections of Tiffany anywhere. Most people are aware of Louis Comfort Tiffany's (1848–1933) ornate lamps, but the varied collection also includes the interior of a Neo-Byzantine chapel, designed by the artist for the World's Exposition in 1893.

Moravian-born sculptor Albin Polasek spent his retirement at his 3-acre (1.2ha) estate close by. His work is scattered around the grounds and the villa is decorated with Polasek's own art collection. At Rollins College, the Cornell Museum of Fine Arts has the oldest fine art collection in the state, comprising European and American paintings and sculpture.

Scenic Boat Tour Operating since the 1930s, this one-hour tour travels across three lakes in Winter Park, passing lakeside mansions, Rollins College and the 11-acre (4.5ha) Kraft Azalea Gardens, a park with impressive flowerbeds.

Central Florida Zoo

To the northeast of Orlando, in Sanford, the Central Florida Zoo aims to educate its visitors about its impressive collection of creatures.

A short history First established as the Sanford Zoo in the 1920s, the Central Florida Zoological Park began with a disparate collection of animals donated by traveling circuses and private owners. Today, as an accredited member of the American Zoo and Aquarium Association, it is a key player in the campaign to maximize the captive populations of several endangered species.

Animals The big cats, including two cheetahs and a breeding pair of clouded leopards, are the highlight of the collection. Siamang apes and mandrills are among the zoo's apes and monkeys, while a playful family of endangered red ruffed lemurs are representative of the smaller mammals. The Herpetarium is the finest captive snake habitat in the city, with examples from the minuscule to the massive; eyelash vipers, king snakes and eastern diamondback rattlesnakes. If snakes aren't cuddly enough, visit Sanford's petting zoo where you can feed a fluffy llama, goats and chickens.

Habitat The zoo's home is prime Florida wetland, which makes a great natural environment for the animals. Exhibits that make the most of the location include the Butterfly Garden and the Backyard Habitat exhibit, where you meet creatures native to the region, and Florida Trek, which leads you into the margins of the wetland.

Watch this space! That's because the zoo has big plans for the next decade, including a Sumatran Tiger Exhibit, a natural range for orangutans, and Zoolab for close encounters with animals.

INFORMATION

➕ Off map
✉ 3755 N US Highway 17-92, Sanford
☎ 407/323-4450
🕐 Daily 9–5
🍴 Café $
♿ Very good
💲 Cheap
❓ Special events and lectures during the year

Boggy Creek Airboat Rides

HIGHLIGHTS

- Riding on the airboat
- Seeing alligators in a natural habitat
- Pristine lakeland scenery
- Huge variety of other wildlife

On one of the most exhilarating rides at Orlando you never get off the ground. It's your chance to play "crocodile hunter," but we don't advise jumping out of the boat like Steve Irwin!

How? The airboat is the perfect vehicle for the central Florida landscape and its numerous lakes and swamps. With the engine above water and a shallow draft it can glide over the vast grass banks that grow around the shallows. And with the engine idling it floats almost silently to get you closer to the wildlife. The US Coast Guard-accredited Master Captains expertly guide you to watch natural behavior in an unspoiled environment.

INFORMATION

- ✚ N11
- ✉ 3702 Big Bass Road, Kissimmee
- ☎ 407/344-9550
- ⊙ Daily, tours every half hour 9–5.30 with longer days during major holidays. Reservations required for night tours
- 🍴 Restaurant $–$$
- ♿ Good
- 💲 Day tours moderate, night tours expensive

Where? East Lake Tohopekaliga is one of the largest and least developed lakes in the Orlando area. This rich environment is home and breeding ground for a diverse range of animals. It's estimated that there are hundreds of alligators of all shapes and sizes, plus turtles, snakes and birds such as bald eagles, herons, ospreys, anhingas, egrets and Sand Hill Cranes.

When? Boggy Creek runs both day and night tours. Day tours last 30 minutes and you'll see a range of wildlife, although there's no guarantee that you'll spot alligators, as they often retreat to remote areas, especially in the middle of the day. Night tours lasting one hour are better for alligator spotting, as the animals are more active after dark. The spotlight on the helmet of your captain will reflect alligators' eyes, but seeing other creatures is less likely in the dark.

ORLANDO's
best

Rides and Roller Coasters

YOU MUST BE AS TALL AS THIS LINE TO RIDE RIVER ADVENTURE

BE AWARE

Most rides and roller coasters have height requirements ranging from 40 inches (1.1m) to 54 inches (1.4m). Some rides can also be dangerous for pregnant women and people with heart conditions. Look for information panels, clearly posted at each ride entrance.

Access for visitors with ambulatory disabilities usually depends on the person's ability to transfer from a wheelchair to the ride, as cast members are not allowed to physically move them.

THE AMAZING ADVENTURES OF SPIDER-MAN®

You are drawn into the drama as Spider-Man hunts for thieves who have stolen the Statue of Liberty. The storyline is simple yet the roller coaster is an amazing combination of exceptional visual effects, track ride and live action, and a drop sequence that will leave you speechless.

✉ Marvel Super Hero Island®, Universal Studios Islands of Adventure™ (➤ 37)

BIG THUNDER MOUNTAIN RAILROAD

Oops! You're on a runaway steam train racing down a mountainside. Not the best coaster for thrills, but the Disney animation and landscaping gives it an edge.

✉ Frontierland, Disney's Magic Kingdom® (➤ 27)

DINOSAUR!

Travel back in time to save the last dinosaur from extinction in this exhilarating combination of coaster and simulator. Optical effects, including the impact of a colossal asteroid, keep the action hot.

✉ DinoLand, Disney's Animal Kingdom® (➤ 26)

DUELING DRAGONS®

An open-air roller coaster, Dueling Dragons® pits two separate inverted rails in opposing directions with close high-speed passes raising adrenaline levels already excited by the longest drop in the park.

✉ The Lost Continent®, Universal Studios Islands of Adventure™ (➤ 37)

THE HAUNTED MANSION

A motorized improvement of the old Haunted House fairground attraction, the fantastic special effects and gruesome antics will shock and surprise those brave enough to enter the Haunted Mansion.

✉ Liberty Square, Disney's Magic Kingdom® (➤ 27)

INCREDIBLE HULK COASTER®

The twists, loops and drops of the

ARE WE HAVING FUN YET?

Right: the Incredible Hulk Coaster at Universal Studios Islands of Adventure™

ultra-fast Hulk are faithful to roller coaster tradition. From the initial blast out of the start gate, it's thrilling to the final second.

✉ Marvel Super Hero Island®, Universal Studios Islands of Adventure™ (▶ 37)

KRAKEN
Orlando's only "floorless" coaster (where riders are restrained at the shoulders with legs dangling), Kraken is also the city's fastest at 65mph (104kph), tallest at 15 stories and longest coaster with seven inversions. This is one to tick off the "must do" list.

✉ SeaWorld (▶ 39)

MEN IN BLACK™ ALIEN ATTACK™
As a MiB agent, your first mission is to save the universe. Throughout the ride you can try to amass points by killing the aliens, which adds enormously to the fun and almost demands that you ride again to improve your score.

✉ Universal Studios Florida™ (▶ 36)

REVENGE OF THE MUMMY™
Based on the *The Mummy* action films, the special effects are on the same scale as the movie with a coaster to propel you bullet-like into the thrills and scares of the 3-D special effects.

✉ New York, Universal Studios Florida™ (▶ 36)

SPACE MOUNTAIN®
Take a ride through the solar system in this totally enclosed coaster. As your mind is fooled into thinking you are in the depths of outer space, the rails lead you into a series of switchback turns and short drops. The speed and visuals make it a great thrill.

✉ Tomorrowland, Disney's Magic Kingdom® (▶ 27)

TERMINATOR 2® 3-D
Not so much a ride as an experience; you'll be in the middle of the action as Cyberdyne Systems seems set to take over the world before the Terminator makes his appearance. This was the first in a new generation of theme park thrills; it still has excellent 3-D effects.

✉ Hollywood, Universal Studios Florida™ (▶ 36)

THE TWILIGHT ZONE TOWER OF TERROR™
A high-tech development of the Haunted Mansion (see above), you begin a tour of this old Hollywood hotel through the lift. In a very short time you'll enter the supernatural Twilight Zone™.

✉ Sunset Boulevard, Disney-MGM Studios (▶ 28)

YOU DON'T NEED TO STAND IN LINE

Both Disney and Universal operate systems that allow you to bypass the lines. Disney's FASTPASS and Universal Express operate in the same way. Insert your park ticket into the machine at the entrance to the given ride and it will issue you with a time to return later in the day (a one hour window) when you will be able to ride almost immediately.

Top: the Revenge of the Mummy at Universal Studios Florida™

Shows and Parades

LA NOUBA

Guy Laliberté elevated circus arts to the level of theater with his company Cirque du Soleil®, an entertaining blend of mime, acrobatics and acting. The La Nouba show has been created especially for Disney and is named after the French phrase "faire la nouba," which means "to live it up." The show has elements of the classic conflict of "good versus evil" and is visually spectacular.

Top: Beetlejuice's Rock 'n' Roll Graveyard Revue™

BEAUTY AND THE BEAST – LIVE ON STAGE

Take a musical journey through this delightful Disney romance as Belle gradually falls in love with the Beast. The stage costumes and scenes are worthy of Broadway, as is the musical score.
✉ Theater of the Stars, Disney-MGM Studios (➤ 28)

BEETLEJUICE'S ROCK 'N' ROLL GRAVEYARD REVUE™

Creepy Beetlejuice invites his ghoulish friends, Dracula, Frankenstein and his bride plus Wolfman, for a soft rock sing-along in this lively stage show.
✉ New York, Universal Studios Florida™ (➤ 36) 🕐 4 shows per day, times vary. See park program

CIRQUE DU SOLEIL® LA NOUBA

This 90-minute show has dance, mime, acrobatics and stunning visuals as the colorful cirque people clash with the dour urbanites for control of the earth.
➕ E9 ✉ Downtown Disney, West Side (➤ 33) ☎ 407/939-7600
🕐 Tue–Sat at 6pm and 9pm 🚻 Excellent 💰 Very expensive (includes entrance to clubs at Downtown Disney)

FANTASMIC!

Mickey reprises his roll as the Sorcerer's Apprentice (from the Disney film *Fantasia*), orchestrating a magnificent display of dancing fireworks, lasers and projected images to a wonderful musical score.
✉ Disney-MGM Studios (➤ 28) 🕐 Evening when park is open late, sometimes two shows per night. See park program

FESTIVAL OF THE LION KING

This show combines circus acts and parades. While

the action and the setting are excellent, it's the film's show tunes that really make the production; everyone knows the words so it becomes a great sing-along.
✉ Camp Minnie-Mickey, Disney's Animal Kingdom® (➤ 26) ⊗ Times vary, see park program

ILLUMINATIONS: REFLECTIONS OF EARTH
Designed to encapsulate the life span of planet Earth, from the "Big Bang" to the present day, it's difficult to follow the thread of this show, so simply enjoy it for the exceptional fireworks display that it is.
✉ World Showcase Lagoon, Epcot® (➤ 29) ⊗ After dark but times vary, see park program

INDIANA JONES™ EPIC STUNT SPECTACULAR!
Want to know how those dangerous action sequences you see on adventure films are really done? Then this is the show for you. Don't try this at home!
✉ Disney-MGM Studios (➤ 28) ⊗ Several shows per day. Times vary so consult your park program

MICKEY'S JAMMIN' JUNGLE PARADE
Winding its way through Africa, Discovery Island® and Asia, Mickey and Minnie join Rafiki, Baloo and others for a party to celebrate the "animal kingdom."
✉ Disney's Animal Kingdom® (➤ 26) ⊗ Afternoon, times vary. Consult your park program

MICKEY'S PHILHARMAGIC
Mickey Mouse has a great adventure with his buddies Donald, Simba, Ariel and Aladdin in this enhanced 3-D film.
✉ Fantasyland, Disney's Magic Kingdom® (➤ 27) ⊗ Several times daily, times change. Consult your park program

SHARE A DREAM COME TRUE PARADE
Dancing along Main Street USA past Cinderella Castle, this mega-parade spins the best of Disney magic into one spectacle. It's great mobile theater.
✉ Disney's Magic Kingdom® (➤ 27) ⊗ Afternoon and early evening parade times vary. Consult your park program

SHREK 4-D™
Lord Farquaard comes back from the dead in an attempt to reclaim his bride, Princess Fiona, from Shrek in this entertaining 4-D (see panel) film show.
✉ Production Central, Universal Studios Florida™ (➤ 36) ⊗ Shows throughout the day

VOYAGE OF THE LITTLE MERMAID
A romantic, musical journey, Voyage of the Little Mermaid is one of Disney's longest running shows. An excellent set and special effects keep it fresh.
✉ Disney-MGM Studios (➤ 28) ☎ Throughout the day, times vary

WHAT IS 4-D?

A new viewing experience, 4-D is, in simple terms, 3-D plus "smell-i-vision" and "action transfer," so that you really feel part of the plot.
To make this idea become reality, Universal contracted Seastar Show FX Inc. to design new theater seats for the Shrek show. In addition to being comfortable, they had to be an integral part of the action. Without giving too many details away, the seats have air and water jets plus the capability to "drop" in time with the screen action. Enjoy!

Shopping Malls

FESTIVAL BAY MALL

Anchored by a multiscreen cinema complex, Festival Bay features unique stores such as Bass Pro Outdoor World, Shepler's Westernwear and Ron Jon's.
🔢 G6 ✉ 5250 International Drive, Orlando ☎ 407/351-7718 🕐 Mon–Sat 10–9, Sun noon–7 🍴 Restaurants $–$$ and cafés $ 🚌 Lynx routes 8, 24 and 42 ♿ Excellent 👊 Free

DISCOUNT COUPONS

Most of the Orlando shopping malls issue books of discount coupons that are accepted in many of their stores (normally with a minimum spend). To obtain yours, visit the customer services kiosk when you arrive and this may save you more than a few dollars on your shopping spree.

THE FLORIDA MALL

Orlando's largest and most well-rounded shopping experience with 5 department stores and more than 250 stores filled with dependable brands.
🔢 J6/7 ✉ 8001 S. Orange Blossom Trail, Orlando ☎ 407/851-6255 🕐 Mon–Sat 10–9, Sun 10–6 🍴 Several restaurants $–$$ and food court $ 🚌 Lynx routes 4, 7, 37, 42, 43 and 52 ♿ Excellent 👊 Free

LAKE BUENA VISTA FACTORY STORES

This open-air mall wraps around its parking lot and has 125 outlet stores including Gap, Old Navy and Fossil. World of Coffee has the best brew in the city.
🔢 E9 ✉ 15591 South Apopka-Vineland Road, Lake Buena Vista ☎ 407/238-9301 🕐 Mon–Sat 10–9, Sun 10–6 🍴 Cafés $ 🚌 Lynx route 304 ♿ Very good 👊 Free

THE MALL AT MILLENIA

This 1.2 million sq ft (111,480 sq m) mall has the finest upscale shopping in the city, with names including Tiffany, Cartier and Chanel.
🔢 G5 ✉ 4200 Conroy Road, Orlando ☎ 407/363-3555 🕐 Mon–Sat 10–9, Sun 12–7 🍴 Restaurants $$ and food court $ 🚌 Lynx routes 24 and 40 ♿ Excellent 👊 Free

ORLANDO PREMIUM OUTLETS MALL

This open-air mall has cut-price designer items from Hugo Boss and Armani, among others, in addition to stores such as Timberland and Nike.
🔢 F9 ✉ 8200 Vineland Avenue, Orlando ☎ 407/238-7787 🕐 Mon–Sat 10–11, Sun 10–9 🍴 Food court $ 🚌 Lynx route 42; I-Ride ♿ Very good 👊 Free

WINTER PARK VILLAGE

The red stucco of this open-air mall gives the feel of a Mediterranean hamlet. Fashion boutiques and gourmet food shops sit beside interior design stores.
🔢 Off map ✉ 480 North Orlando Avenue (US 17/92) ☎ 407/671-4343 🕐 Shops Mon–Sat 10–9, Sat noon–6. Eateries longer hours 🍴 Several restaurants $–$$ and café $ 🚌 Lynx routes 1, 9, 14, 16, 23 and 39 ♿ Very good 👊 Free

Getting in Touch with Animals

AIRBOAT YOU RIDE

Rent your own family-size (four adults or two adults and three children) airboat and head into the cypress swamps north and south of I-192 where you may see alligators, herons, egrets and otters. You can rent canoes or electric boats for a quieter approach.

✚ G11 ✉ 4266 West Highway 192, Kissimmee ☎ 407/847-3672 🕐 Daily 9–5 (weather permitting) 🚌 Lynx routes 55 and 56 ♿ Good 💲 Cheap (boats by the hour)

DIVE QUEST

Immerse yourself in this 6-million gallon, tropical "Living Seas" aquarium where you can swim among turtles, eagle rays and brown sharks, in front of other Disney visitors. Certified divers only.

✉ The Living Seas, Future World, Epcot® ☎ 407/939-8687 🕐 Two sessions per day 💲 Very expensive (separate ticket to Epcot entry – no necessity to buy an Epcot ticket)

GREEN MEADOWS PETTING FARM

The low-tech, but hands-on, Green Meadows is set in natural farmland, complete with a shady, tropical canopy. The two-hour tours allow you to milk a cow, take a donkey ride and get close to pigs, geese and chickens. It's a change of pace from the hectic parks.

✚ Off map ✉ 1368 South Poinciana Boulevard, Kissimmee ☎ 407/846-0770 🕐 Daily 9am, last tour at 4pm 🍴 Vending machines ♿ Good 💲 Moderate

KEEPER FOR A DAY

Work behind the scenes with dolphin keepers and help with the feeding and care of these intelligent mammals, plus other sea life and the birds. You'll also take part in animal training and playtime.

✉ Discovery Cove (➤ 40) 💲 Very expensive (includes all Discovery Cove activities and Dolphin interactive experience plus ticket to SeaWorld)

REPTILE WORLD SERPENTARIUM

Find out how to milk a snake at one of the United States' biggest snake farms, with 50 species. The snakes have to be "milked" regularly to collect their venom so that it can be used in anti-venom.

✚ Off map ✉ 5705 East Irlo Bronson Highway, St. Cloud ☎ 407/892-6905 🕐 Tue–Sun 9–5.30. Snakes milked at noon and 3pm 🍴 Vending machines ♿ Good 💲 Cheap

HOW IT WORKS

Snake venom is a form of saliva that is pumped into the flesh through hollow fangs when the victim is bitten. When a snake is milked (this is harmless to the snake), its venom is injected in small harmless doses into another animal (usually a horse). Over time the horse's blood develops antibodies that fight the poison. Doctors collect the plasma from the horse's blood to create anti-venom to neutralize the poison and save the lives of human snakebite victims.

Above: handling an alligator at Boggy Creek Airboat Rides

Places to get Wet

DON'T CATCH A COLD

During the hot Florida summers, water rides are a favorite way to cool down, but between November and April when temperatures don't hit the 90s Fahrenheit (30s Centigrade), children may become cold and dispirited if exploring the parks in wet clothing. Take a dry set and leave them in a locker, just in case.

BLIZZARD BEACH

The concept: After a freak snowstorm, someone builds Florida's first ski resort. The weather hots up and the melting snow creates some superb rides, such as Summit Plummet, the longest water slide in the country at 120ft (36m) and speeds of 60mph (96kph).
➕ B10 ✉ Buena Vista Drive, Lake Buena Vista ☎ 407/560-3400 🕐 Core hours 10–6, longer in summer 🍴 Range of cafés $–$$ 🚌 Lynx route 56 ♿ Excellent 💲 Expensive

JURASSIC PARK RIVER ADVENTURE®

A cruise through tranquil Jurassic countryside goes wrong and culminates in the longest, fastest and deepest drop of any water ride in Orlando.
✉ Jurassic Park, Universal Studios Islands of Adventure™ (➤ 37)

KALI RIVER RAPIDS®

Take a white-water rafting trip down a tropical river. With water flowing freely over the rocks, every ride is different. One thing is certain, you'll get wet!
✉ Disney's Animal Kingdom® (➤ 26)

THE SHAMU® SHOW

Killer whale Shamu® is the symbol of SeaWorld. His show is the highlight of the park, not least for the traditional soaking the audience receives every time his massive body breaks the water.
✉ SeaWorld (➤ 39)

Above: Wet 'n' Wild

WATERMANIA

This 36-acre (14ha) water park doesn't have the high octane rides of other parks. However, it does have the great advantage of shady woodland where you can enjoy a picnic – bring your own food (no glass).
➕ D11 ✉ 6073 West Irlo Bronson Highway ☎ 407/396-2626 or 800/527-3092 🕐 Open Mar–Sep, daily 10–5; Sep, Mon–Fri 10–5, Sat–Sun 11–5; Oct shorter hours. Closed Nov–Mar 🍴 Café $ 🚌 Lynx routes 55 and 56 ♿ Very good 💲 Expensive

WET 'N' WILD

Wet 'n' Wild has some seriously thrilling water rides. There's something here for the whole family, with multiperson tube rides and a half-mile surf drag.
➕ G6 ✉ 6200 International Drive ☎ 407/351-1800 or 800/992-WILD 🕐 Core hours 10–5, open as late as 11pm on summer weekends 🍴 Cafés $ 🚌 Lynx routes 8, 21, 38 and 42; I-Ride ♿ Very good 💲 Expensive

To Tee Off

CHAMPIONSGATE

Championsgate boasts two renowned Greg Norman-designed courses. The International is a British-style links course with sandy rough to tax the wayward. Featuring in many golfing "best of" surveys, it's the home of the David Leadbetter Golf Academy. The National course curves through strands of citrus groves and sports some challenging bunkers.
🏌 Off map ✉ 1400 Masters Boulevard ☎ 407/787-4653 or 888/558-9301 🕐 Tee times sunrise until 90 mins before sunset 🍴 Full service restaurant SS–SSS ♿ Excellent 💰 Very expensive

GRAND CYPRESS GOLF CLUB

With 45 holes playable from the club house, golfers can enjoy several days of play here. The courses are only open to guests of Grand Cypress resort. The New Course harks back to the traditional Scottish links, while others are pure American styling.
🏌 D8 ✉ 1 North Jacaranda ☎ 407/239-4700 or 877/330-7277 🕐 Tee times sunrise until 90 mins before sunset 🍴 Several full service restaurants SS–SSS ♿ Excellent 💰 Very expensive

GRANDE LAKES

This diverse 18-hole, par-72 course was designed by Greg Norman and routed through typical Florida wetland and forest environments. It culminates in the shadow of the luxury of the Ritz-Carlton and Marriott hotels. There are exceptional practice areas, and the usual Ritz Carlton 5-star service.
🏌 H8 ✉ The Ritz-Carlton Golf Club, 4048 Central Florida Parkway ☎ 407/393-4900 🕐 Tee times sunrise until 90 mins before sunset 🍴 Restaurant SSS 🚌 Lynx route 43 ♿ Excellent 💰 Very expensive

PALM GOLF COURSE

Disney's best course plays host to the annual, televised, PGA Tour FUNAI Classic tournament. Designed by Joe Lee, it is renowned for its hazards including several plays over water. It has an excellent practice range.
🏌 B8 ✉ 1950 West Magnolia/Palm Drive, Lake Buena Vista ☎ 407/939-4653 🕐 Tee times sunrise until 90 mins before sunset 🍴 Café S–SS 🚌 Lynx route 302 ♿ Excellent 💰 Very expensive

PANTHER LAKE

Voted one of America's Top 10 public courses, Panther Lake is a well-rounded 18 holes with excellent well-conditioned greens among native wetlands and pine and oak forest.
🏌 A7 ✉ 16301 Phil Ritson Way, Winter Garden ☎ 407/656-2626 or 888/PAR-3672 🕐 Tee times sunrise until 90 mins before sunset 🍴 Restaurant SS–SSS ♿ Excellent 💰 Very expensive

LOWER YOUR HANDICAP

We can only scratch the surface of greater Orlando's 125 golf courses, so for further and detailed information on the finest greens, required handicaps, fees and other details log on to **www.orlandogolf.com** or contact the Orlando Convention and Visitors Bureau for their GolfOrlando leaflet.

Above: perfect your drive at one of Orlando's 125 golf courses

Views

57TH ST.

This backlot trompe-l'oeil set puts you right in the heart of New York. Wander around and get some interesting new perspectives.

✉ Universal Studios Florida™ (➤ 36)

HOT AIR BALLOON FLIGHT

From around 1,000ft (305m) up, you can get amazing views across Orlando and the theme parks, though the exact course depends on wind direction. Florida's lakes, swamps and golf courses are equally fascinating from the air. The following companies offer flights:

ORANGE BLOSSOM BALLOONS

🎌 A10 ✉ P.O. Box 22908 Lake Buena Vista. Departure point La Quinta Hotel, 7769 West Irlo Bronson Highway at Maingate ☎ 407/239-7677 🕓 Daily 6am (weather permitting) 🍴 Breakfast included in ticket price 🚫 None 💲 Very expensive

UP, UP AND AWAY

On any balloon ride, a member of the crew will be commandeered to unfold and inflate the balloon canopy and ready the basket. After the landing you'll help deflate the balloon and fold it safely away. Once this is achieved there'll be a champagne toast to welcome you into the ballooning fraternity.

Above: watching the sunrise from an Orange Blossom Balloon

BLUE WATER BALLOONS

🎌 E9 ✉ P.O. Box 560572, Orlando. Departure point Perkins Restaurant at junction I4 with the 535 at Lake Buena Vista ☎ 407/894-4050 or 800/586-1884 🕓 Daily, one hour before sunrise (weather permitting) 🍴 Breakfast included in ticket price 🚫 None 💲 Very expensive

INTERNATIONAL DRIVE AT NIGHT

A riot of neon as the sun begins to set, this is Americana at its best. Look north from Sand Lake Road or south from the bend at Magical Midway for the best views.

🎌 F6 ✉ International Drive 🕓 Nightly after sunset 🍴 Range of cafés S and full service restaurants $$–$$$ 🚫 Good 💲 Free

MAIN STREET USA

Surely one of the most photographed vistas in the world, the avenue that bisects Disney's Magic Kingdom leads the eye directly to Cinderella Castle. It couldn't be more picture perfect.

✉ Disney's Magic Kingdom® (➤ 27)

SKYTOWER

This 400ft (120m) needle offers views across the park and beyond to the Central Florida flatlands. The six-minute, enclosed ride offers a 360-degree rotation of the upper level before returning you gently to earth.

✉ SeaWorld 💲 Cheap (in addition to SeaWorld entrance ticket)

Children

ADVENTURE GOLF

Mini-golf is transformed into a scenic escapade at a venues around I-Drive, Lake Buena Vista and Maingate. The courses's themed landscapes may include volcanoes and live, albeit young, alligators.

CONGO RIVER ADVENTURE GOLF

➕ F7 ✉ 6312 International Drive ☎ 407/352-0042 🕐 Daily 10–10 🍴 Vending machines $ 🚌 Lynx routes 8, 38 and 42; I-Ride mainline stop 18 ♿ Few 💲 Cheap

FANTASYLAND

You'll find all Disney's characters here, so it's the perfect place for children to meet Snow White, Dumbo or Peter Pan. The rides are generally gentle and make a great introduction to the roller coasters children can enjoy when they get older (and taller).
✉ Disney's Magic Kingdom® (➤ 27)

FUNSPOT ACTION PARK

Away from the high-tech wizardry of the major theme parks there are low-tech funfairs for children to enjoy (Old Town ➤ 32, Magical Midway on International Drive ➤ 34). The best is Funspot Action Park, with 4 go-kart tracks, 8 family rides and a covered arcade.
➕ G6 ✉ 5551 Del Verde Way ☎ 407/363-3867 🕐 Daily 10am–midnight 🍴 Café $ 🚌 Lynx routes 8, 24 and 42; I-Ride ♿ Good 💲 Expensive unlimited daily rides or cheap per ride

SEUSS LANDING

Immerse your children in the pastel-colored world of Dr. Seuss. All their favorite characters are here and the rides are designed for them.
✉ Universal Studios Islands of Adventure™ (➤ 37)

VANS SKATEPARK

This indoor and outdoor environment is for skaters and skateboarders with chutes, pipes and jumps and an area for beginners. All equipment can be rented.
➕ G6 ✉ Festival Bay Mall, 5250 International Drive ☎ 407/351-3881 🕐 Daily 10–10 🍴 Café $ 🚌 Lynx routes 8, 24 and 42; I-Ride ♿ Very good 💲 Moderate

WHO WAS DR. SEUSS?

Theodore Seuss Geisel began his career as a cartoonist before moving into children's literature. His first manuscript Mulberry Street received 27 rejections before being published. He developed his characteristic syntax in response to a call to help make learning to read fun for children. The first title, *The Cat in the Hat*, was an international bestseller. At the time of his death Giesel, as Dr. Seuss, had sold 200 million books in 15 languages and helped children all over the world understand the wonder of the written word.

Below: the Caro Seussel at Universal Studios Islands of Adventure™

Free

Above: you can buy orchids at the World of Orchids

A WORLD OF ORCHIDS

An extensive collection of orchids from around the world can be viewed here, along with rescued tropical birds. You can buy blooms and have them shipped home.

✚ Off map ✉ 2501 Old Lake Wilson Road ☎ 407/396-1887 ◷ Daily 10–5 ♿ Good ▯ Free

EOLA PARK

A stroll around Lake Eola is the place to meet Orlando suburbanites. They'll be jogging, walking their dogs or feeding the geese. There are concerts throughout the summer in the small arena, or take a gondola ride on the lake.

✚ K3 ✉ Downtown, corner of Robinson Street, Rosalind Avenue, Central Boulevard and Summerlin Avenue ◷ Open 24 hours ▮ Hue restaurant and a range of cafés $–$$ ◻ Lynx routes 5, 6, 15 and 39 ♿ Good ▯ Free

HERE COME THE DUCKS

The Peabody tradition began in the 1930s when some mischievous hunters placed live ducks (in those days used as decoys for hunting) in the fountain of the Peabody hotel in Memphis. They were an instant hit with guests and each hotel now has its own feathered residents. Today's ducks work in several teams and rotate between hotel duties and a free-range life on a Florida farm. In deference to their place in hotel life, no duck meat is served in any Peabody hotel restaurant.

MARCH OF THE DUCKS

Every Peabody hotel has a family of ducks, (one male and four females). They spend the nights in luxury in their own duck "palace" and their days in the lobby bar fountain on the first floor. People flock to watch them arrive at the fountains in the morning and troop back to the "palace" in the afternoon, accompanied by the stirring music of John Philip Souza

✚ F7 ✉ Peabody Hotel, 9801 International Drive ☎ 407/352-4000 ◷ Daily, ducks arrive at 11am and depart at 5pm ▮ Restaurants $$–$$$ and bar/café $ ◻ Lynx routes 8, 38 and 42; I-Ride ♿ Excellent ▯ Free

MERCADO

This Mediterranean-style entertainment and shopping complex hosts free live music every night in the central square. It's a great option to start off your evening if you are staying along I-Drive.

✚ F7 ✉ 8445 International Drive ☎ 407/345-9337 ◷ Entertainment starts at 7.30pm ▮ Restaurants $–$$$, cafés $ and food court $ ◻ Lynx routes 8, 38 and 42; I-Ride ♿ Good ▯ Free

SEMINOLE COUNTY HISTORICAL MUSEUM

The history of Seminole County (northern Orlando) is brought to life in this museum of artifacts donated by the local community. It's an interesting journey through the development of central Florida and the people who made it happen.

✚ Off map ✉ 300 Bush Boulevard, Sanford ☎ 407/665-2489 ◷ Mon–Fri 9–5, Sat 9–4 ◻ Lynx route 39 ♿ Very good ▯ Free

ORLANDO
where to...

Character Dining

PRICES

Expect to pay per person for a meal, excluding drinks

$ = up to $12
$$ = $12–$25
$$$ = more than $25

HAIL THE MOUSE

Despite several decades of Disney success, Mickey Mouse is the character every visitor wants to meet, whatever their age. Perhaps it is because the cheerful and ever optimistic rodent spans the age range, having debuted in an early talkie in 1928. Today Mickey is still going strong with his own TV show on the Disney Channel. He's omnipresent at Disney parks around the world. As Walt once said "…never lose sight of one fact… That this was all started by a mouse."

CINDERELLA'S GALA FEAST, 1900 PARK FARE $$$

You'll meet different characters at this buffet. Check the daily notice-board, but the usual timetable is breakfast with Mary Poppins and dinner with Cinderella.
➕ B8 ✉ Disney's Grand Floridian Resort, 4401 Grand Floridian Way, Lake Buena Vista ☎ 407/939-3463 🕐 Breakfast, dinner 🚌 Lynx route 302

CINDERELLA'S ROYAL TABLE $$

Enjoy a buffet breakfast with Disney characters – Cinderella, Snow White, Belle and Aladdin.
➕ B8 ✉ Cinderella Castle, Magic Kingdom ☎ 407/939-3463 🕐 Breakfast 🚌 Lynx routes 50, 56 and 302

CRYSTAL PALACE AT MAIN STREET $$–$$$

Pooh, Eeyore, Piglet and Tigger will join you for a raucous buffet breakfast, lunch or dinner.
➕ B8 ✉ Main Street, Magic Kingdom ☎ 407/939-3463 🕐 Breakfast, lunch, dinner 🚌 Lynx routes 50, 56 and 302

CHEF MICKEY'S $$

Dine with Mickey, Minnie, Goofy and Pluto. There's lots of audience participation.
➕ B8 ✉ Disney's Contemporary Resort, 4600 North World Drive, Lake Buena Vista ☎ 407/939-3463 🕐 Breakfast 7–11, dinner 5–9.30 🚌 Lynx route 302

COMIC STRIP LANE $

Dagwood, Hagar the Horrible and Krazy Cat are some of the cartoon characters featured here.
➕ F6 ✉ Universal Islands of Adventure ☎ 407/363-8000 🕐 10am–park closes 🚌 Lynx routes 21, 37 and 40

DINE WITH AN ASTRONAUT $$$

Chat with an astronaut active in today's space program and learn all about coping with life in space.
➕ Off map ✉ Kennedy Space Center, NASA Parkway FL, 32899 ☎ Ticket line 321/449-4400 🕐 Daily lunch

DINE WITH SHAMU® $$$

At this buffet-style meal beside the killer whale's pool, Shamu® trainers will be answering questions, and you can watch training sessions.
➕ F8/G8 ✉ SeaWorld, 7007 SeaWorld Drive ☎ 407/351-3600 or 800/327-2420 🕐 4.15pm–7.15pm 🚌 Lynx routes 8, 43 and 50; I-Ride

GARDEN GRILL $$$

The perfect place for a taste of Disney magic in the least "Disneyesque" park. The grill is graced with the presence of Mickey and Donald.
➕ C9 ✉ The Land, Futureworld, Epcot ☎ 407/939-3463 🕐 Lunch or dinner 🚌 Lynx routes 301 and 303

LIBERTY TREE TAVERN $$$

Dinner with Mickey, Minnie, Donald and Chip 'n' Dale. Your meal is brought to your table for you to serve the family, rather than being buffet style.
➕ B8 ✉ Magic Kingdom ☎ 407/939-3463 🕐 Dinner 🚌 Lynx routes 50, 56 and 302

Fast Food

AUSTIN COFFEE AND FILM $
Voted the best café in Orlando, the coffee, salads, sandwiches and pastries are fresh.
➕ Off map ✉ 929 West Fairbanks Avenue, Winter Park ☎ 407/975-3364 ⏰ Breakfast, lunch, dinner 🚍 Lynx routes 1, 9 and 16

B-LINE DINER $–$$
A menu of old-fashioned favorites such as hot dogs and apple pie, plus modern healthy choices.
➕ F7 ✉ Peabody Hotel, 9801 International Drive ☎ 407/345-4460 ⏰ 24 hours 🚍 Lynx routes 8, 38 and 42; I-Ride

BUBBALOU'S BODACIOUS BAR-B-QUE $
Try delicious barbequed meats and ribs or the exceptional hot sandwiches.
➕ Off map ✉ 1471 Lee Road, Winter Park ☎ 407/628-1212 ⏰ Lunch, dinner 🚍 Lynx route 23

JOHNNY ROCKETS $
Sit in indoor booths or at chrome tables in the atrium at this '50s-style diner. Excellent burgers and all-day breakfasts are served to a rock-and-roll soundtrack.
➕ G5 ✉ Mall at Millennia, 4200 Conroy Road ☎ 407/903-1006 ⏰ Breakfast, lunch, dinner 🚍 Lynx routes 24 and 40

LULU'S BAIT SHACK $–$$
This casual Cajun–American eatery specializes in "black-ened" meat or fish and has a lively bar at weekends.
➕ F7 ✉ Pointe*Orlando, 9101 International Drive ☎ 407/351-9595 ⏰ Lunch, dinner 🚍 Lynx routes 8, 38 and 42; I-Ride

MACDONALD'S $
The World's Largest MacDonald's has an entertainment area, as well as burgers and healthier menu options.
➕ F6 ✉ 6875 Sand Lake Road, Orlando ☎ 407/351-2158 ⏰ 24 hours 🚍 Lynx routes 8, 21, 38 and 42; I-Ride

MEL'S DRIVE IN $–$$
Themed on the diner in the film *American Graffiti*, Mel's serves authentic burgers, hot dogs and milk shakes.
➕ F6 ✉ Universal Studios ☎ 407/363-8000 ⏰ During park hours 🚍 Lynx routes 21, 37 and 40

THE SCI-FI DINE-IN THEATER RESTAURANT $
Waitstaff on roller skates bring classic American fast food at this '50s-style diner. Burgers and hot dogs are the most popular dishes. Black-and-white sci-fi clips are your entertainment.
➕ C10/11 ✉ Disney-MGM Studios, Buena Vista Drive, Lake Buena Vista ☎ 407/824-4321 ⏰ During park hours 🚍 Lynx route 303

SONIC $
A menu of hotdogs and burgers along with wraps and hot sandwiches is delivered to your table, or your car by a carhop.
➕ G6 ✉ 5399 International Drive ☎ 407/352-0016 ⏰ Breakfast, lunch, dinner 🚍 Lynx routes 8, 38 and 42; I-Ride

EVERYONE LOVES BUBBALOU'S!

Voted best BBQ restaurant in 2004 by the readers of the *Orlando Weekly*, Bubbalou's has some delicious genuine southern dishes and sides on their menu. Try catfish, pulled pork, collard greens, okra and corn bread washed down with root beer or Dr. Pepper.

Surf and Turf

HOW DO YOU LIKE IT?

A good steak depends on many factors, including the animal's diet, the aging process of the meat and the cut. One thing's for sure, if it's not cooked to your liking, it's going to spoil your enjoyment. Here are the terms you'll need to know.

Rare – brown exterior; raw, cold interior

Medium rare – brown exterior; warm red center

Medium – brown except for a small hot-pink interior

Medium well – no pink interior but a little juice

BLUEZOO $$$

Todd English brings you a menu of exceptional seafood dishes from around the globe in this contemporary, neon-lit restaurant and lounge.

◫ C9 ✉ Walt Disney World Dolphin Resort, 1500 Epcot Resorts Boulevard, Lake Buena Vista ☎ 407/934-1111 ◔ Dinner ▣ Lynx route 303

CAPRICCIO GRILL $$$

Mouth-watering steaks are the signature dishes. Other options include chicken and seafood. The trattoria-style dining room has a lively atmosphere.

◫ F7 ✉ Peabody Hotel, 9801 International Drive ☎ 407/345-4450 ◔ Dinner ▣ Lynx routes 8, 38 and 42; I-Ride

CHARLEY'S STEAK HOUSE $$$

Meat is specially selected, aged and then cut in-house and cooked over oak at this family-owned steak house.

◫ F7 ✉ 8255 International Drive ☎ 407/363-0228 ◔ Dinner ▣ Lynx routes 8, 38 and 42; I-Ride

FISHBONES $$–$$$

With a superb selection of market-fresh fish and seafood, this is the place for lobster and Florida stone crab. Steaks come courtesy of Charley's (see above).

◫ G6 ✉ 6707 Sand Lake Road ☎ 407/352-0135 ◔ Dinner ▣ Lynx routes 8, 21, 38 and 42; I-Ride

FISH ON FIRE $–$$

The tasty barbequed seafood and meat is popular with locals at this informal eatery close to the airport.

◫ L6 ✉ 7937 Daetwyler Drive ☎ 407/812-6881 ◔ Lunch, dinner ▣ Lynx route 52

KRES $$–$$$

Contemporary urban styling and great steaks draw a mainly young urban clientele. The lounge is a popular place to relax in the evenings.

◫ J3 ✉ 17 West Church Street ☎ 407/447-7950 ◔ Mon–Fri lunch, dinner, Sat dinner ▣ Lynx route 20

MCCORMICK AND SCHMICK'S $$–$$$

The menu changes twice daily to reflect what is market fresh, but always includes 30 types of seafood. The bar stocks a good range of single malt whiskies.

◫ G5 ✉ Mall at Millenia, Conroy Road ☎ 407/226-6515 ◔ Lunch, dinner ▣ Lynx routes 24 and 40

PALM $$–$$$

Enjoy excellent steak and chops, and the cartoons on the walls of this offshoot of the New York Palms.

◫ F6 ✉ Hard Rock Hotel, Universal Studios ☎ 407/503-DINE (3463) ◔ Mon–Fri lunch, dinner; Sat–Sun dinner ▣ Lynx routes 21, 37 and 40

TEXAS DE BRAZIL $$

Tuck into skewers of your favorite meat grilled to perfection at this authentic Brazilian "churrascaria" (meat restaurant).

◫ G6 ✉ 5259 International Drive ☎ 407/355-0355 ◔ Dinner ▣ Lynx routes 8, 38 and 42; I-Ride

A Gourmet Experience

ARTHUR'S 27 $$$

The Continental cuisine has to be good to outdo the views from 27 stories above Walt Disney World® Resort.

🔲 D/E9 ✉ Wyndham Palace Resort and Spa, Walt Disney World® Resort ☎ 407/827-3450 🕐 Dinner 🚌 Lynx routes 300 and 304

ARTIST POINT $$$

Get a taste of America's northwest with Pacific salmon, buffalo and elk, plus regional wines. The decor is inspired by Frank Lloyd Wright.

🔲 C8 ✉ Disney's Wilderness Lodge ☎ 407/939-3462 🕐 Dinner 🚌 Lynx route 302

ATLANTIS $$$

Atlantis's award-winning menu concentrates on fine seafood, served in an intimate Victorian-style dining room.

🔲 F8 ✉ Renaissance Orlando Resort at SeaWorld, 6677 Sea Harbor Drive ☎ 407/351-5555 🕐 Dinner 🚌 Lynx routes 8, 50

LA BOHEME $$$

Refined European and North American dishes are served here. Sunday's Jazz Brunch is a downtown institution.

🔲 K3 ✉ Westin Grand Bohemian Hotel, 325 South Orange Avenue ☎ 407/313-9000 🕐 Daily breakfast, lunch, dinner, Sun brunch 🚌 Lynx routes 3, 6, 7, 11, 13, 18, 51 and 200; Lymmo

CHEF JUSTIN'S AT PARK PLAZA GARDENS $$$

A protégé of Wolfgang Puck, Justin Plank presents a wonderful, seasonal menu. There's a less expensive but no less delicious menu for the terrace café.

🔲 Off map ✉ 319 Park Avenue South, Winter Park ☎ 407/645-2475 🕐 Lunch, dinner, Sun brunch 🚌 Lynx routes 1, 9 and 23

MANUEL'S ON 28TH $$$

Head downtown for this "foodies" paradise. The modern cuisine has to compete with views from the Bank of America building's 28th floor.

🔲 J/K3 ✉ 390 North Orange Avenue ☎ 407/246-6580 🕐 Tue–Sat dinner 🚌 Lynx 3, 6, 7, 11, 13, 18, 51, 200; Lymmo

NORMANS $$$

Chef Norman Van Aken is one of the founding fathers of "New World Cuisine," so taste the best of his flavors here.

🔲 H8 ✉ Ritz Carlton Hotel, Grande Lakes, 4000 Central Florida Parkway ☎ 407/393-4333 🕐 Dinner 🚌 Lynx route 43

THE PLANTATION ROOM $$$

Fresh ingredients are given a contemporary American twist at this elegant eatery.

🔲 Off map ✉ Celebration Hotel, 700 Bloom Street, Celebration ☎ 407/566-6002 🕐 Breakfast, lunch, dinner

VICTORIA AND ALBERT'S $$$

Enjoy exceptional North American cuisine with a seven-course gourmet fixed menu with wines.

🔲 B8 ✉ Grand Floridian Resort, Floridian Way, Lake Buena Vista ☎ 407/939-3463 🕐 Dinner 🚌 Lynx route 302

POETRY ON THE PLATE

"Walt Whitman was probably the first poet to leap forth with a distinct American voice. To many he did not seem European enough in cadence or manner…Whitman was an object of passion scorned by traditionalists. In the end his mark was made because he fused the ancient and revered body of poetry with the radically new "body electric." The mark will also be made for those who are daring enough to meld the good and old cooking with the good and new cooking."
Norman Van Aken, Orlando chef

Celebrity Connections

EMERIL FACTS

Things you may not know about celebrity chef Emeril Lagasse:

● He spent his childhood in Fall River, Massachusetts

● After graduation he was offered a music scholarship

● He opened his first restaurant Emeril's in New Orleans in 1990

● In 1999 he was named as one of *People Magazine's* "Most Intriguing People of the Year"

● His seven cookbooks have sold over 3.5 million copies

● He reaches 78 million households with his TV shows "The Essence of Emeril" and "Emeril Live"

BONGO'S CUBAN CAFÉ $$

Musicians Gloria and Emelio Estefan bring a taste of Cuba to Florida. The restaurant, in a pineapple-shaped building, evokes 1950s Cuba.

✛ D/E9 ✉ Downtown Disney Westside ☎ 407/828-0999 🕐 Lunch, dinner 🚌 Lynx routes 300, 301, 302, 303 and 304

DM $$–$$$

American football hero Dan Marino brings classics such as seared tuna and beef steaks to Pointe*Orlando.

✛ F7 ✉ Point*Orlando, 9101 International Drive ☎ 407/363-1013 🕐 Lunch, dinner 🚌 Lynx routes 8, 38 and 42; I-Ride

EMERIL'S $$$

Chef Emeril Lagasse resurrected the Cajun/Creole cuisine of New Orleans. Try his sauces on chicken, meat and andouille sausage.

✛ F6 ✉ 6000 Universal Boulevard, CityWalk ☎ 407/224-2424 🕐 Lunch, dinner 🚌 Lynx routes 21, 37 and 40

HARD ROCK CAFÉ $$

The largest in this chain of cafés, Hard Rock Orlando also has its most in-depth collection of rock memorabilia.

✛ F7 ✉ CityWalk ☎ 407/351-7625 🕐 Lunch, dinner 🚌 Lynx routes 21, 37 and 40

MARGARITAVILLE $–$$$

Crooner Jimmy Buffet offers his take on the Caribbean with cocktails and simple yet delicious food. Buffet's music plays during the day and he sometime puts in a live appearance.

✛ F7 ✉ CityWalk, 6000 Universal Boulevard ☎ 407/224-2155 🕐 Lunch, dinner 🚌 Lynx routes 21, 37 and 40

THE MURRAY BROS. CADDYSHACK $$

Comedian Bill Murray and his brothers worked as caddies to pay their way through school. His Caddyshack comedy was the starting point of their restaurant chain.

✛ G6 ✉ Festival Bay Mall, 5250 International Drive ☎ 407/351-3848 🕐 Lunch, dinner 🚌 Lynx routes 8, 24, 42; I-Ride

NASCAR® CAFÉ $–$$

This official NASCAR restaurant has great cars outside and memorabilia inside. Burgers, salads and sandwiches are on the menu.

✛ F7 ✉ CityWalk ☎ 407/224-RACE (7223) 🕐 Breakfast, lunch, dinner 🚌 Lynx routes 21, 37 and 40

NBA CITY $–$$

Shoot some hoops in the basketball area then eat burgers, pasta or pizza.

✛ F7 ✉ 6860 Universal Boulevard, CityWalk ☎ 407/363-5919 🕐 Lunch, dinner 🚌 Lynx routes 21, 37 and 40

PLANET HOLLYWOOD $–$$

Some of the best Hollywood and film memorabilia is on show here, with a full menu of standard burgers, grilled entrées and sandwiches.

✛ D/E9 ✉ Downtown Disney, Buena Vista Drive, Lake Buena Vista ☎ 407/827-STAR (7827) 🕐 Lunch, dinner 🚌 Lynx routes 300, 301, 302, 303 and 304

American Staples – Franchises

BAHAMA BREEZE $–$$
The Caribbean menu and live music makes this a popular venue for families and a younger crowd later in the night.
🔲 F7 ✉ 8849 International Drive ☎ 407/248-2499 🕐 Lunch, dinner 🚌 Lynx routes 8, 38 and 42; I-Ride

BENNIGANS $–$$
A great place for family dining, Bennigans is styled on a traditional Irish bar and grill. The menu includes snacks.
🔲 F7 ✉ 6324 International Drive ☎ 407/351-4435 🕐 Breakfast, lunch, dinner 🚌 Lynx routes 8, 38, 42; I-Ride

THE CHEESECAKE FACTORY $–$$
This chain is renowned for its vast menu (with 50 cheesecakes) and huge portions.
🔲 G5 ✉ 4200 Conroy Road (at Mall at Millennia) ☎ 407/226-0333 🕐 Lunch, dinner 🚌 Lynx routes 24 and 40

KOBE JAPANESE STEAK HOUSE $–$$
Come here for noisy teppanyaki or a quieter sushi bar. The signature Kobe steak is aged then massaged with Japanese gin.
🔲 E9 ✉ 8460 Palm Parkway, Lake Buena Vista ☎ 407/239-1119 🕐 Lunch, dinner 🚌 Lynx routes 300 and 304

OLIVE GARDEN $–$$
Close ties with Italy and a discerning eye for ingredients means the American/Italian food is always tasty here.
🔲 G5 ✉ 4101 Conroy Road ☎ 407/345-8331 🕐 Lunch, dinner 🚌 Lynx routes 24 and 40

OUTBACK STEAK HOUSE $–$$
The no-nonsense styling of Australia's outback eateries complements the fuss-free steaks and grilled meats.
🔲 Off map ✉ 3109 West Vine Street, Kissimmee ☎ 407/931-0033 🕐 Lunch, dinner 🚌 Lynx routes 10, 50 and 56

RAINFOREST CAFÉ $–$$
The jungle canopies and animated wildlife of these cafés make them an exciting setting for a family meal of burgers, pizzas and steaks.
🔲 D/E9 ✉ Downtown Disney, East Lake Buena Vista Drive ☎ 407/939-3463 🕐 Lunch, dinner 🚌 Lynx routes 300, 301, 302, 303 and 304

RED LOBSTER $–$$
Affordable seafood and shellfish cooked any way you want it, including tasty linguini.
🔲 G6 ✉ 3936 International Drive ☎ 407/351-0033 🕐 Lunch, dinner 🚌 Lynx routes 8, 38, and 42; I-Ride

SIZZLERS $
There's relaxed family-style eating with buffet breakfast and starter bar at excellent prices here.
🔲 F7 ✉ 9142 International Drive ☎ 407/351-5369 🕐 Breakfast, lunch, dinner 🚌 Lynx routes 8, 38, 42; I-Ride

TONY ROMA'S THE PLACE FOR RIBS $–$$
Succulent ribs in Roma's sauce are the main reason for dining here.
🔲 F7 ✉ 8560 International Drive ☎ 407/248-0094 🕐 Lunch, dinner 🚌 Lynx routes 8, 38 and 42; I-Ride

European and Mediterranean Options

DELICIOUS AND NUTRITIOUS

Mediterranean cuisine is considered one of the healthiest in the world, resulting in a lower level of disease (certain cancers and heart disease) and a longer life span. What all these national cuisines have in common is a base of olive oil, delicious fresh salads and seasonal vegetables, a high proportion of seafood and an accompanying glass of red wine.

ANAELLE & HUGO $$$
One of the best new restaurants in Orlando, its Mediterranean menu has a wide range of options and the pastries have a loyal following. Good wine list.
🚼 F6 ✉ 7533 West Sand Lake Road ☎ 407/996-9292 🕙 Lunch, dinner, Sun brunch 🚌 Lynx route 43

BRIO TUSCAN GRILLE AND BAKERY $$
An up-to-date twist on the old Italian trattoria, Brio serves great breads and pizza from its ovens. There's a terrace for eating alfresco.
🚼 Off map ✉ Winter Park Village, Orange Avenue, Winter Park ☎ 407/622-5611 🕙 Lunch, dinner 🚌 Lynx routes 1, 9, 14, 16, 23 and 39

CAFÉ DE FRANCE $$$
This intimate bistro serves excellent French cuisine, including the Gallic specialties of foie gras and snails.
🚼 L1 ✉ 526 Park Avenue South, Winter Park ☎ 407/647-1869 🕙 Lunch Tue–Sat, dinner Mon–Sat 🚌 Lynx routes 1, 9, 23

CITRICO'S $$
Featuring a menu of northern Mediterranean dishes from France, Italy and Spain with pastas and risottos.
🚼 B8 ✉ Disney's Grand Floridian Resort, 4401 Grand Floridian Way, Lake Buena Vista ☎ 407/939-3463 🕙 Dinner Wed–Sun 🚌 Lynx route 302

COLUMBIA RESTAURANT $$
One of Florida's oldest restaurants, Columbia serves tasty Spanish/Cuban food such as paella, tapas and tender roast pork. Dine outside in a shady courtyard.
🚼 Off map ✉ 649 Front Street, Celebration ☎ 407/566-1505 🕙 Lunch, dinner

LE COQ AU VIN $$–$$$
Great French restaurant with seasonal menu changes, but always the eponymous signature dish. Simple decor and a good wine selection.
🚼 K5 ✉ 4800 South Orange Avenue ☎ 407/851-6980 🕙 Tue–Fri lunch, dinner; Sat–Sun dinner 🚌 Lynx routes 7, 11 and 18

RESTAURANT MARRAKESH $$–$$$
Moroccan cuisine with great couscous and spit-roasted lamb. Decor is authentic, but you sit at tables, not on the floor.
🚼 C9/10 ✉ Morocco, World Showcase, Epcot ☎ 407/939-3463 🕙 Lunch, dinner 🚌 Lynx routes 301 and 303

PRIMO $$–$$$
Contemporary Italian cuisine featuring organic ingredients from the restaurant's own garden. Unusual options include edible flowers in salads.
🚼 H8 ✉ Marriott Hotel, Grande Lakes, 4000 Central Florida Parkway ☎ 407/393-4444 🕙 Dinner 🚌 Lynx route 43

SPOODLES $$$
Spoodles's menu raids the Mediterranean. Italian or Greek salads could precede a French or Spanish entrée.
🚼 C10 ✉ Disney's Boardwalk Resort, Lake Buena Vista ☎ 407/939-3463 🕙 Breakfast, lunch, dinner 🚌 Lynx route 303

Asian, Pacific and Fusion

CAFÉ TU TU TANGO $$
The mix-and-match menu features dishes from the Mediterranean, Caribbean, South America and the Pacific.
✚ F7 ✉ 8625 International Drive ☎ 407/248-2222 🕐 Lunch, dinner 🚌 Lynx routes 8, 38 and 42; I-Ride

DAKSHIN $–$$
Voted "Best Indian" restaurant by the *Orlando Weekly*, Dakshin serves southern Indian cuisine that includes a range of interesting vegetarian options.
✚ E9 ✉ 12541 State Road 535 ☎ 407/827-9080 🕐 Lunch, dinner, Sun brunch 🚌 Lynx route 304

EMERIL'S TCHOUP CHOP $$$
Emeril's latest Orlando venture melds Pacific and Oriental flavors to produce delicious stir-fries and salads plus inventive entrées.
✚ F6 ✉ Royal Pacific Resort, Universal Studios, 6300 Hollywood Way ☎ 407/503-2467 🕐 Lunch, dinner

HUE $$$
One of the hottest spots in the downtown area, Hue offers contemporary Florida cuisine in a very modern setting.
✚ K3 ✉ 629 East Central Boulevard, Thornton Park ☎ 407/849-1800 🕐 Lunch, dinner 🚌 Lynx routes 5 and 6

RAN-GETSU OF TOKYO $–$$$
This stylish Japanese restaurant has excellent authentic cuisine and a very good menu at the city's longest sushi bar.
✚ F7 ✉ 8400 International Drive ☎ 407/345-0044 🕐 Lunch, dinner 🚌 Lynx routes 8, 38 and 42; I-Ride

ROY'S $$–$$$
Roy's Hawaiian fusion cuisine concentrates on fresh seafood accented by delicious sauces and marinades. The sea bass is a signature dish.
✚ F6 ✉ 7760 Sand Lake Road ☎ 407/352-4844 🕐 Dinner 🚌 Lynx route 43

SAMBA ROOM $$–$$$
An Asian/Latin America fusion menu matches meat and fish with fruits and spices at this large dining room.
✚ F6 ✉ 7468 West Sand Lake Road ☎ 407/226-0550 🕐 Mon–Fri lunch, dinner, Sat–Sun dinner 🚌 Lynx routes 21, 43

THAI THANI $$
Thai dishes, with the spiciness toned down for Western palates, are served in a traditionally decorated dining room. If you enjoy it hot, tell your server. The tom yam is recommended.
✚ G8 ✉ 11025 International Drive ☎ 407/239-9733 🕐 Lunch, dinner 🚌 Lynx route 8; I-Ride

WOLFGANG PUCK GRAND CAFÉ $–$$$
Four eateries in one complex means casual to upscale choices. The fine dining features Chef Wolfgang Puck's Asian/Californian dishes.
✚ D/E9 ✉ Downtown Disney West Side, Buena Vista Drive, Lake Buena Vista ☎ 407/938-9653 🕐 Lunch, dinner 🚌 Lynx routes 300, 301, 302, 303, 304

WHAT IS "FUSION" CUISINE?

One definition is the "integrating at disparate styles and ingredients" (Wikipedia), where culinary traditions from more than one culture or geographical region are blended. This new fashion was born as mass travel created a more informed restaurant clientele at the same time as the client base in many urban areas became more culturally diverse.

Fusion cuisine was innovated in California, but soon took hold in multicultural metropolitan areas such as Miami, Vancouver (Canada) and Sydney (Australia).

Disney Shopping

ARE THOSE BAGS HEAVY?

All the major theme parks operate a system that allows you to forward any souvenir purchases to a central point to collect as you leave, so you don't need to carry them around all day with you.
If you are staying at a Walt Disney World® Resort hotel, any purchases made in any of their theme parks will be delivered to your hotel room while you continue to enjoy the rides and shows.

COUNTY BOUNTY

This is a great shop for young fans to spend their allowance on Mickey and Minnie stuff without being distracted by souvenirs aimed at older shoppers.
✚ B8 ✉ Mickey's Toontown Fair, Magic Kingdom ☎ 407/824-4321 🚌 Lynx routes 50, 56 and 302

DISNEY CHARACTER PREMIER

Official Disney end-of-line merchandise mixed with full-price items.
✚ G6/7 ✉ Belz Factory Outlet World, Mall 1 Unit 47, 5401 West Oakridge Road ☎ 407/354-3255 🚌 Lynx routes 8, 38 and 42; I-Ride

DISNEY CHARACTER PREMIER

A further opportunity to buy Disney merchandise outside the parks. Seasonal and line-end items predominate.
✚ F9 ✉ Unit 1252, Orlando Premium Outlet Mall, 8200 Vineland Avenue ☎ 407/477-0222 🚌 Lynx route 42; I-Ride

DISNEY CHARACTER WAREHOUSE

Another official Disney outlet store with high-quality souvenirs at lower-than-park prices.
✚ G6/7 ✉ Belz Factory Outlet World, Mall 2 Unit 109–110, 5401 West Oakridge Road ☎ 407/345-5285 🚌 Lynx routes 8, 38 and 42; I-Ride

DISNEY PIN TRADERS

Start a collection, trade for better or sell at this marketplace for Disney pin collectors.
✚ D/E9 ✉ Downtown Disney Marketplace, Lake Buena Vista Drive, Lake Buena Vista ☎ 407/828-3800 🚌 Lynx routes 300, 301, 302, 303 and 304

DISNEY'S WONDERFUL WORLD OF MEMORIES

"Scrap booking" is coming back into fashion and here you'll find lots of affordable ways to create a personal remembrance of your Disney visit, including files, stickers and stationery.
✚ D/E9 ✉ Downtown Disney Marketplace, Lake Buena Vista Drive, Lake Buena Vista ☎ 407/828-3058 🚌 Lynx routes 300, 301, 302, 303 and 304

EMPORIUM

This the Disney "one stop shop" for a comprehensive range of merchandise.
✚ B8 ✉ Main Street USA, Magic Kingdom ☎ 407/824-4321 🚌 Lynx routes 50, 56 and 302

MITZI'S HALLMARK

A specialist in Walt Disney classic souvenirs and limited editions, Mitzi's also stocks Lladro and Swarovski figures.
✚ E9 ✉ Crossroads Mall, Route 535 at I-4 ☎ 407/827-1075 🚌 Lynx route 300

WORLD OF DISNEY

The largest official Disney store outside the parks and reputedly the largest in the world. Whatever souvenir you are looking for, you should find it here.
✚ D/E9 ✉ Downtown Disney Marketplace, Lake Buena Vista Drive, Lake Buena Vista ☎ 407/828-3800 🚌 Lynx routes 300, 301, 302, 303 and 304

Universal Studios Stores

ALL THE BOOKS YOU CAN READ

All of Dr. Seuss's rhyming stories can be found here in print or CD/DVD so you can revisit these zany couplets or introduce them to the younger generation.

✚ F6 ✉ Seuss Landing, Islands of Adventure ☎ 407/224-5800 🚌 Lynx routes 21, 37 and 40

CARTOONIVERSAL

Pick up original cartoon celluloids and other original Nickelodeon artwork featuring Scooby, Spider-Man and others, or copies and prints for a few dollars less.

✚ F6 ✉ CityWalk ☎ 407/363-8000 🚌 Lynx routes 21, 37 and 40

DINOSTORE(SM)

There's a whole range of "dino" related merchandise here, from the serious scientific and educational material for would-be archaeologists to fun stuff.

✚ F6 ✉ Jurassic Park, Islands of Adventure ☎ 407/224-5800 🚌 Lynx routes 21, 37 and 40

THE MARVEL ALTERNIVERSE

Merchandise for all your favorite Marvel comic characters can be found here, all under one roof.

✚ F6 ✉ Marvel Super Hero Island, Islands of Adventure ☎ 407/224-5800 🚌 Lynx routes 21, 37 and 40

MIB GEAR

Buy Men in Black-themed souvenirs including the signature black sunglasses and replica ray guns.

✚ F6 ✉ World Expo, Universal Studios ☎ 407/224-5800 🚌 Lynx routes 21, 37 and 40

NICKSTUFF

Fans of Spongebob Squarepants and Jimmy Neutron should find enough to keep them happy here, with merchandise on Universal's latest TV heroes.

✚ F6 ✉ Production Central, Universal Studios ☎ 407/224-5800 🚌 Lynx routes 21, 37, 40

UNIVERSAL STUDIOS OUTLET

You'll find slightly cheaper and end-of-line goods at this Universal store. It's a good place to bargain hunt, but won't have the full range to choose from.

✚ G5/6 ✉ Belz Factory Outlet World, Mall 1 Unit 5, 5401 West Oakridge Road ☎ 407/354-0126 or 407/351-5576 🚌 Lynx routes 8, 38 and 42; I-Ride

UNIVERSAL STUDIOS STORE

A great place to shop if you don't want to enter the Universal parks. A good range of Universal and Islands of Adventure merchandise.

✚ F6 ✉ CityWalk, Universal Boulevard ☎ 407/363-8000 🚌 Lynx routes 21, 37 and 40

UNIVERSAL STUDIOS STORE

A comprehensive range of Universal souvenirs is found on the main thoroughfare close to the entrance/exit.

✚ F6 ✉ Plaza of the Stars, Universal Studios ☎ 407/224-5800 🚌 Lynx routes 22, 37, 40

A MARVELOUS HISTORY

Marvel heroes arrived in the 1940s when Human Torch and Submariner fought the Nazi's. In the 1950s, the publishers fell foul of the McCarthy Trials, but during the early '60s, The Fantastic Four, The Incredible Hulk and Spider-Man were launched. By the late 1960s Marvel Comics cartoons hit TV screens.

In the 1970s the X-Men, Conan the Barbarian and Red Sonja were introduced and the Incredible Hulk moved into live-action television with a highly successful series. The late 1990s saw Marvel elevated to the big screen with X-Men the Movie and Spider-Man.

More "Themed" Merchandise

SOMETHING MORSE

Louis Comfort Tiffany, son of a silversmith, trained as an artist and developed an interest in the chemistry of glass. In 1881 he patented a glass that amalgamated several colors to produce myriad hues. By 1885 he was producing his signature pieces. His primary source of inspiration was nature; hence his lamps reveal a metal stem with shade glass leaves and blossoms. Tiffany was one of the first American artists to reach a worldwide audience, being particularly appreciated in the Paris of the art nouveau and art deco era.

GATORLAND

Since alligators are no longer a protected species you'll find gator skin boots and hats, plus gator heads for sale in the gift shop. The "gator" theme continues throughout this large store, with fluffy toys and kitsch items.
➕ J10 ✉ 14501 South Orange Blossom Trail ☎ 407/855-5496 🚌 Lynx route 4

KENNEDY SPACE CENTER

The most expensive souvenirs here are the NASA leather jackets, but there are affordable items: dehydrated astronaut meals, posters, books and DVDs.
➕ Off map ✉ State Road 405, FL 32899 ☎ 321/449-4444

LA NOUBA

Beguiled by the graceful aerial performances? Buy original artworks, themed items or DVDs to relive the show.
➕ D/E9 ✉ Downtown Disney Marketplace, Lake Buena Vista Drive, Lake Buena Vista ☎ 407/939-1298 🚌 Lynx routes 300, 301, 302, 303 and 304

LEU GARDENS

A veritable treasure trove for the keen gardener, including books, small tools and themed ornaments and collectibles.
➕ K2 ✉ 1920 North Forest Avenue ☎ 407/246-2620 🚌 Lynx routes 2 and 13

MEDIEVAL TIMES

Some imaginative gifts here, including suits of armor and handmade swords. Kids will love glow-in-the-dark sword and shield sets.
➕ Off map ✉ 4510 Irlo Bronson Memorial Highway, Kissimmee ☎ 407/239-0214 🚌 Lynx routes 55 and 56

MORSE MUSEUM

A good range of Tiffany and Arts and Crafts copies, plus prints and miniatures. Books on artistic styles and genres and gifts such as picture frames and jewelry are also available.
➕ L1 ✉ 445 Park Avenue North, Winter Park ☎ 407/645-5311 🚌 Lynx routes 1, 9 and 23

ORLANDO MUSEUM OF ART

You'll find books, prints and copies of "objets d'art" in this gift shop. Many items reflect the shows and permanent exhibits.
➕ K2 ✉ 2416 North Mills Avenue ☎ 407/896-4321 🚌 Lynx routes 1, 9 and 39

ORLANDO SCIENCE CENTER

A small gift shop with affordable items, but also educational games.
➕ K2 ✉ 777 East Princeton Street ☎ 407/514-2000 🚌 Lynx routes 1, 9 and 39

SEAWORLD

You'll find themed merchandise at each of the "habitats," though huge fluffy Shamu® soft toys are the souvenir of choice. SeaWorld's Waterfront area has other shops selling clothing and jewelry.
➕ F/G8 ✉ SeaWorld, 7007 SeaWorld Drive ☎ 1 800/327-2420 or 407/351-3600 🚌 Lynx routes 8 and 50

Mainstream Brands

ANN TAYLOR

Classical suburban styling for women. Clothing and accessories for work, play and the evening with the accent on feminine, but not starchy.

➕ K1 ✉ 126 Park Avenue North, Winter Park ☎ 407/628-5600 🚌 Lynx routes 1, 9, 23

BANANA REPUBLIC

Casual fashion clothing for men, women and children. Conservative street styling.

➕ F9 ✉ Unit 400, Orlando Premium Outlet Mall, 8200 Vineland Avenue ☎ 407/239-7741 🚌 Lynx route 42; I-Ride

BASS & CO

Footwear and clothing for the family with the emphasis on comfortable fashion.

➕ F9 ✉ Unit 900, Orlando Premium Outlet Mall, 8200 Vineland Avenue ☎ 407/238-2563 🚌 Lynx route 42; I-Ride

GUESS

Young and vibrant street wear and accessories for men and women.

➕ J5/6 ✉ Florida Mall, 8001 South Orange Blossom Trail ☎ 407/888-9880 🚌 Lynx routes 4, 7, 37, 42 and 52

LEVI'S® OUTLET BY DESIGN

Levi's denim jeans are an American icon and its range of modern styles offers something for all body shapes.

➕ G5/6 ✉ Belz Factory Outlet World Mall 2, Unit 102, Factory Outlet World ☎ 407/352-3118 🚌 Lynx routes 8, 38, 42; I-Ride

NINE WEST

This season's footwear and accessories to accent current fashions.

➕ G6/7 ✉ Florida Mall, 8001 South Orange Blossom Trail ☎ 407/859-5455 🚌 Lynx routes 4, 7, 37, 42 and 52

OLD NAVY OUTLET

Founded in 1994, Old Navy offers great value casual clothing such as Ts, sweats and pants in classic styles.

➕ J6/7 ✉ Lake Buena Vista Factory Stores, 15661 Apopka Vineland Road ☎ 407/238-0493 🚌 Lynx route 300

TIMBERLAND

Timberland started with rugged footwear, but its growing retail empire also features clothing and outerwear.

➕ G5/6 ✉ Belz Factory Outlet World, Annex Unit 72, 5401 West Oakridge Road ☎ 407/370-6630 🚌 Lynx routes 8, 38 and 42; I-Ride

TOMMY HILFIGER

The American success story of the last 20 years (see panel), Tommy Hilfiger offers what he calls "classic styling with a twist," bringing the East Coast look within the price range of the average shopper.

➕ F9 ✉ Unit 200, Orlando Premium Outlet Mall, 8200 Vineland Avenue ☎ 407/628-5600 🚌 Lynx route 42; I-Ride

VICTORIA'S SECRET

Beautiful women's lingerie, swimwear and nightwear with everything from the sexy to the practical.

➕ J6/7 ✉ Florida Mall, 8001 South Orange Blossom Trail ☎ 407/859-9983 🚌 Lynx routes 4, 7, 37, 42 and 52

TOMMY HILFIGER

The latest and perhaps greatest success story in American fashion, Tommy Hilfiger was born in 1951 as one of nine children. He began his retail empire with one store in his native northeast and began designing under his label "Tommy" in 1984.

In 1994 performer Snoop Dogg wore a Tommy shirt on an appearance on Saturday Night Live, kick-starting a stellar rise in demand. Today sales of Tommy clothing top $2 billion per year and Hilfiger is a major influence on urban high-street styling in the US.

Designer Labels

A LITTLE EXTRA

The Florida state legislature applies a tax to all sales within its territory and this is currently 6 percent. This amount does not appear on the price label. It is added to your purchase price at the register.

AX ARMANI EXCHANGE

You'll find great end-of-line items from this energetic fashion empire at this outlet store.

🚻 F9 ✉ Unit 1122, Orlando Premium Outlet Mall, 8200 Vineland Avenue ☎ 407/550-4490 🚌 Lynx route 42; I-Ride

CHANEL

French couture at its best from the house that reinvented fashion, with the Coco handbags and matching footwear.

🚻 G5 ✉ The Mall at Millennia, 4200 Conroy Road ☎ 407/352-5100 🚌 Lynx routes 24 and 40

FURLA

This Italian, family-run company produces high-quality leather shoes, bags and accessories to accompany your favorite outfit.

🚻 G5 ✉ Mall at Millennia, 4200 Conroy Road ☎ 407/226-9155 🚌 Lynx routes 24 and 40

GUCCI

Italian style designed by one of the most famous names in fashion. The off-the-peg fashions are supported by shoes and accessories, such as the Gucci belts and bags.

🚻 G5 ✉ Mall at Millennia, 4200 Conroy Road ☎ 407/903-1033 🚌 Lynx routes 24 and 40

HUGO BOSS

The world-renowned German fashion design house brings Teutonic styling to Florida.

🚻 G5 ✉ Mall at Millennia, 4200 Conroy Road ☎ 407/345-8889 🚌 Lynx routes 24 and 40

JIMMY CHOO

The most sought-after shoes of the last decade, Jimmy Choos make an exceptionally sexy statement and can only be found in a few outlets in the US.

🚻 G5 ✉ The Mall at Millennia, 4200 Conroy Road ☎ 407/352-6310 🚌 Lynx routes 24 and 40

KENNETH COLE

American design house with classic lines for men and women, plus a full range of accessories for your full seasonal wardrobes.

🚻 G5 ✉ The Mall at Millennia, 4200 Conroy Road ☎ 407/352-5300 🚌 Lynx routes 24 and 40

OFF 5TH – SAKS FIFTH AVENUE OUTLET

This upscale New York department store dispatches end-of-line and unsold seasonal stock to Belz so you could pick up a bargain.

🚻 G5/6 ✉ Belz Designer Outlet Centre, Unit 19, 5211 International Drive ☎ 407/354-5757 🚌 Lynx routes 8, 38 and 42; I-Ride

POLO RALPH LAUREN FACTORY STORE

The relaxed "preppy" style of Ralph Lauren polo clothing for the whole family comes at a discount price here.

🚻 G5/6 ✉ Belz Designer Outlet Centre, Unit 1, 5211 International Drive ☎ 407/352-3632 🚌 Lynx routes 8, 38 and 42; I-Ride

ZEGNA

Outlet store of this stylish European fashion house for men.

🚻 F9 ✉ Unit 1153, Orlando Premium Outlet Mall, 8200 Vineland Avenue ☎ 407/550-4490 🚌 Lynx route 42; I-Ride

Household Goods

THE BRASS BAZAAR
Authentic homeware from Morocco, including fantastic rustic pottery, turned brassware and inlaid wooden items.
✚ C9/10 ⊠ Morocco, World Showcase, Epcot ☎ 407/824-4321 🚍 Lynx route 301

LINEN 'N' THINGS
An excellent range of bedding, bed linens, towels and pretty accessories for the home.
✚ G5 ⊠ Millennia Plaza, 4625 Millenia Way ☎ 407/226-2669 🚍 Lynx routes 24 and 40

ONEIDA
The world's largest producer of stainless steel and silver plated goods, Oneida can make your dining table look beautiful with cutlery, goblets and vases. Also sells accompanying tableware.
✚ G5/6 ⊠ Belz Factory Outlet World, Mall 2, Unit 146, 5401 West Oakridge Road ☎ 407/351-6337 🚍 Lynx routes 8, 38 and 42; I-Ride

POTTERY BARN
A treasure trove of fashionable accessories for every room in your home, from furniture to throws and rugs to prints and pictures.
✚ J6/7 ⊠ Florida Mall, 8001 South Orange Blossom Trail ☎ 407/850-9128 🚍 Lynx routes 4, 7, 37, 42 and 52

ROYAL DOULTON
Beautiful quality English china and glass, including one-of-a-kind items and collectible patterned table services.
✚ G5/6 ⊠ Belz Factory Outlet World 1, Unit 10, 5401 West Oakridge Road ☎ 407/345-1417 🚍 Lynx routes 8, 38 and 42; I-Ride

WATERFORD/ WEDGWOOD
Two world-renowned names, Wedgwood for its quality porcelain and Waterford for its cut lead crystalware. Stock up on the items you'll use for important social and family occasions.
✚ G5/6 ⊠ Belz Designer Outlet Centre, Unit 17, 5211 International Drive ☎ 407/351-5353 🚍 Lynx routes 8, 38 and 42; I-Ride

WILLIAMS-SONOMA
Excellent shop selling "kitchenalia", including gadgets, crockery, linens and cooking accessories.
✚ L1 ⊠ 142 Park Avenue, Winter Park ☎ 407/628-5900 🚍 Lynx routes 1, 9 and 23

YANKEE CANDLE COMPANY
Good-quality candles and home fragrances, plus accessories such as candlesticks and table-ware are sold here.
✚ J6/7 ⊠ Florida Mall, 8001 South Orange Blossom Trail ☎ 407/826-4800 🚍 Lynx routes 4, 7, 37, 42 and 52

YONG FENG SHANGDIAN STORE
A wide range of crafts and household goods from China, the finest of which are authentic silk rugs and carpets from 1ft (0.3m) long to 12ft (3.5m) long. Prices are high, but so is quality.
✚ C9/10 ⊠ China, World Showcase, Epcot ☎ 407/824-4321 🚍 Lynx route 301

WEIGHING IN
If you're flying home, remember to check your luggage allowance before you start spending. These bargains are awfully tempting, but with most airlines limiting check-in baggage to two bags per passenger (max weight for each bag 32kg) and excess baggage charged at $110 (Delta Airlines in 2005) or £70 per bag (Virgin Atlantic 2005) it could add an unwelcome expense at the end of your trip.

Sports Clothing and Equipment

THE BIRTH OF THE MODERN RUNNING SHOE

Bill Bowerman had been a prolific athlete in his youth and returned from World War II to take over the sports programs at the University of Oregon. During a trip to New Zealand he saw people running just for fun. He imported the idea to the US under the epithet – jogging! A couple of years later he was inspired to invent a new running shoe by the dimples in his breakfast waffle; the sculpted shape increased traction and this is what gave Nike shoes the edge!

ADIDAS

Since the 1920s Adidas has been producing sports equipment; it's now one of the world's leading brand names.
G6 4949 International Drive 407/370-9606 Lynx routes 8, 38, 42; I-Ride

BASS PRO SHOPS OUTDOOR WORLD

This store is the place for your fishing, hunting and camping supplies – you can even buy live bait from vending machines when the store is closed. The clothing and footwear is great for the Florida climate and outdoor pursuits.
G6 Festival Bay Mall, 5156 International Drive 407/563-5200 Lynx routes 8, 38 and 42; I-Ride

EDWIN WATTS GOLF

Everything for the rookie or regular golfer, including clubs, balls, footwear and a choice of colorful golf apparel.
F7 8330 South International Drive 407/351-1444 or 800/874-0146 Lynx routes 8, 38 and 42; I-Ride

EVERYTHING BUT WATER

Swimsuits and bikinis for all shapes and ages. Two-piece swimwear can be bought separately for differing hip and bust sizes.
G5 Mall at Millennia, 4200 Conroy Road 813/871-5918 Lynx routes 24 and 40

FOOTLOCKER

A range of end-of-line and sports footwear for however you get active.
G5/6 Belz Factory Outlet World, Mall 1, Unit 60, 5401 West Oakridge Road 407/352-0804 Lynx routes 8, 38 and 42; I-Ride

NIKE

A leading American sporting company for serious athletic gear and fashion-led sportswear.
F9 Orlando Premium Outlet Mall, Vineland Avenue 407/239-3663 Lynx route 42; I-Ride

REEBOK

Outdoor and sports footwear and clothing with replica kits of American and European sporting teams.
F7 8747 International Drive 407/370-3570 Lynx routes 8, 38, 42; I-Ride

RON JON SURF SHOP

The East Coast legend brings his surfing world to Orlando. Buy boards and other equipment, plus the latest surfwear.
G6 Festival Bay Mall, 5160 International Drive 407/481-2555 Lynx routes 8, 38 and 42; I-Ride

SPORTS DOMINATOR

You can't miss this store with its huge fiberglass statues of sportsmen on the facade. It's a great place to compare brands and buy team outfits.
F6 6464 International Drive 407/354-2100 Lynx routes 8, 38, 42; I-Ride

VANS SKATEPARK

A good range of skates, boards, plus protective gear and clothing.
G6 Festival Bay Mall, 5220 International Drive 407/351-3881 Lynx routes 8, 38 and 42; I-Ride

Collectibles and Americana

ANTIQUES ROW

A diminutive district of around 25 shops, but worthwhile for lovers of antiques such as "kitchenalia," arts and crafts items and 20th-century collectibles.

✚ K2 ✉ North Orange Avenue (between Princeton Street and Magnolia Street) 🚍 Lynx routes 1, 9 and 14

THE BLACK SHEEP

A fantastic repository for lovers of needlecraft, this shop sells a vast range of silks and wools patterns and books. It also provides instruction.

✚ L1 ✉ 128 Park Avenue, Winter Park ☎ 407/644-0122 🚍 Lynx routes 1, 9 and 23

CULINARY COTTAGE

A delightful historic house c1870 with three floors of decorative accessories and collectibles for the home, plus beauty products and jewelry.

✚ Off map ✉ 141 West Church Avenue, Longwood ☎ 407/834-7220

HOLLYWOOD CLASSICS

From film memorabilia movie posters to a range of unusual gift items for the enthusiastic collector.

✚ G6 ✉ Festival Bay Mall, 5250 International Drive ☎ 407/903-1818 🚍 Lynx routes 8, 24 and 42; I-Ride

ORLANDO HARLEY-DAVIDSON

You may not be able to fit a motorcycle into your suitcase, but try a leather jacket, key fob, die cast model, watch or, if all else fails, a T-shirt

that displays your love of this American classic.

✚ H4 ✉ Historic Factory Dealership, 3770 West 37th Street ☎ 407/423-0346 🚍 Lynx routes 24 and 303

SCOTT LAURENT COLLECTION

This gallery sells what are set to be the collectibles of tomorrow with present-day art, crafts and sculptures.

✚ L1 ✉ 348 Park Avenue North, Winter Park ☎ 407/629-0278 🚍 Lynx routes 1, 9, 23

SHEPLERS

The widest range of Western ware in the city with a great choice of leather cowboy boots, jackets and hats.

✚ G6 ✉ Festival Bay Mall, 5232 International Drive ☎ 407/563-1063 🚍 Lynx routes 8, 24 and 42; I-Ride

STARABELIAS

One of the largest memorabilia emporia in the States, this shop has a huge collection of autographs, historical and celebrity objects. You can have articles shipped worldwide.

✚ D/E9 ✉ Downtown Disney West Side, 1502 East Buena Vista Drive ☎ 407/859-8489 🚍 Lynx routes 300, 301, 203, 303 and 304

TAGS WITH CLASS

Have your own laser car registration tags printed with amusing messages or anecdotes. You can also buy laser key rings.

✚ D11 ✉ Unit 303, Old Town, 5775 West US Highway 192, Kissimmee ☎ 407/390-7277 or 1 800/819-TAGS (8247) 🚍 Lynx routes 55 and 56

QUILTING

Antique quilts are one of the most precious and beautiful artifacts of the American collectibles market. Squares of fabric sewn together by hand to traditional patterns, they were first and foremost practical articles for the homesteaders of the 18th and 19th centuries.

Today, quilting has undergone an immense revival, with communal commemorative quilts being produced in remembrance of AIDS suffers, the victims of the 9/11 terrorist attack and the soldiers who didn't return from the war in Iraq.

Live Performances

WHAT'S ON

In the free newspaper *Orlando Weekly* you'll find comprehensive entertainment listings in categories from live music to sports events to exhibitions.
The monthly *Orlando Magazine* offers articles about what's new and hot around the city so you can pick on the city vibe, but its listings are limited to the major events and exhibitions.

ADVENTURERS' CLUB

Based on gentlemen's clubs of the 1930s, the Adventurers' Club offers tales of exploration.
🚇 D/E9 ✉ Pleasure Island, Downtown Disney, 1590 Buena Vista Drive, Lake Buena Vista ☎ 407/828-3025 🕐 Daily 7pm–2am 🚌 Lynx routes 300, 301, 302, 303 and 304

BOB MARLEY – A TRIBUTE TO FREEDOM

Listen to live reggae music nightly in the open-air gazebo.
🚇 F6 ✉ CityWalk, 1000 Universal Studios Plaza ☎ 407 /224-3663 🕐 Daily 4pm–2am 🚌 Lynx routes 21, 37 and 40

CITYJAZZ

There's nightly live soul, jazz and R&B at Cityjazz. Thursdays are comedy club evenings.
🚇 F6 ✉ CityWalk, 1000 Universal Studios Plaza ☎ 407/224-2189 🕐 Sun–Thu 8pm–1am, Fri–Sat 7pm–2am 🚌 Lynx routes 21, 37 and 40

THE COMEDY WAREHOUSE

Sanitized stand-up "improv" comedy, as expected from Disney.
🚇 D/E9 ✉ Pleasure Island, Downtown Disney, 1590 Buena Vista Drive, Lake Buena Vista ☎ 407/828-3025 🕐 5 shows nightly Thu–Sat, 4 shows Sun–Wed 🚌 Lynx routes 300, 301, 302, 303 and 304

HOUSE OF BLUES

Live acts, a great brunch and special guests make House of Blues a must for music lovers.
🚇 D/E9 ✉ Pleasure Island, Downtown Disney, 1490 Buena Vista Drive, Lake Buena Vista ☎ 407/934-BLUE (2583) or

2222 🕐 Mon–Thu 8.30pm, Fri–Sun 9.30pm 🚌 Lynx routes 300, 301, 302, 303 and 304

IMPROV COMEDY CLUB

Guest stand-ups and regular amateur nights at this popular venue.
🚇 J3 ✉ 129 West Church Street ☎ 321/281-8000 🕐 Nightly from 7pm 🚌 Lynx routes 20, 22 36, 40

JELLYROLLS

The resident pianists at this club, named after "Jelly Roll" Morton, take requests.
🚇 C10 ✉ Disney Boardwalk, Epcot Resorts Boulevard, Lake Buena Vista ☎ 407/939-1500 🕐 7pm–2am 🚌 Lynx 303

LATIN QUARTER

Live Latino sounds to tango the night away. Also a disco dance floor.
🚇 F6 ✉ CityWalk, Universal Studios Plaza ☎ 407/224-FOOD (3663) 🕐 Nightly 7pm–2am 🚌 Lynx routes 21, 37 and 40

PLEASURE ISLAND JAZZ COMPANY

Live jazz sessions from local talent range from "improv" to progressive.
🚇 D/E9 ✉ Pleasure Island, Downtown Disney, 1590 Buena Vista Drive, Lake Buena Vista ☎ 407/828-3025 🕐 7pm–2am 🚌 Lynx routes 300, 301, 302, 303 and 304

THE SOCIAL

Bands at Orlando's top downtown live music venue cover all genres of popular music. Over 21s.
🚇 J/K3 ✉ 54 North Orange Avenue, Orlando address ☎ 407 /246-1419 🕐 Sat–Thu 8pm–2am, Fri 5pm–2am 🚌 Lynx routes 3, 6, 7, 11, 13, 18, 51, 200

Clubs

8TRAX

A true '70s disco harking back to Saturday Night Fever, with sounds such as Chic, Tavares and Earth Wind and Fire.

✚ D/E9 ✉ Pleasure Island, Downtown Disney, 1590 Buena Vista Drive, Lake Buena Vista ☎ 407/828-3025 🕐 7pm–2am 🚌 Lynx routes 300, 301, 302, 303 and 304

ANTIGUA

Dance club with several bars and lounges for drinks and full-blown dance sessions. Antigua has a Caribbean theme, with a tropical fish tank, but plays electronic and house music. Over 18s.

✚ J3 ✉ 41 West Church Street ☎ 407/649-4270 🕐 Mon–Thu 3pm–10pm, Fri–Sun 3pm–2am 🚌 Lynx routes 20, 22, 36, 40

BET SOUNDSTAGE CLUB

Home of the finest R&B and soul music.

✚ D/E9 ✉ Pleasure Island, Downtown Disney, 1590 Buena Vista Drive, Lake Buena Vista ☎ 407/828-3025 🕐 Nightly 7pm–2am 🚌 Lynx routes 300, 301, 302, 303 and 304

BLUE ROOM

This longstanding Orlando venue was re-launched in the early 2000s. DJs play dance music. Over 21s.

✚ J3 ✉ 17 West Pine Street ☎ 407/843-2583 🕐 Wed–Sat 9pm–3am 🚌 Lynx routes 3, 6, 7, 11, 13, 18, 51 and 200; Lymmo route

COWBOYS

The premier country nightclub of the region; you can line dance all evening. Live events and all-age evenings.

✚ J4 ✉ 1108 South Orange Blossom Trail ☎ 407/422-7115 🕐 Thu–Sat 8pm–2am 🚌 Lynx routes 4 and 8

THE GROOVE

The best in dance music from the '70s to today, The Groove caters to age groups 20s to 50s.

✚ F6 ✉ CityWalk, Universal Boulevard Plaza ☎ 407/224-8000 🕐 Daily 9pm–2am 🚌 Lynx routes 21, 37 and 40

MANNEQUIN'S DANCE PALACE

Mannequin's revolving dance floor is the place to enjoy the latest rock and pop. The leading dance club at Pleasure Island. Over 18s Sun–Wed, over 21s Thu–Sat.

✚ D/E9 ✉ Pleasure Island, Downtown Disney, 1590 Buena Vista Drive, Lake Buena Vista ☎ 407/828-3025 🕐 Nightly 7pm–2am 🚌 Lynx routes 300, 301, 302, 303 and 304

MATRIX

A big-bucks light show and the city's largest dance floor make Matrix unique. Dance to techno and trance. Over 18s.

✚ F7 ✉ Pointe*Orlando, 9101 International Drive ☎ 407/370-3700 🕐 Wed–Sun 9pm–2am 🚌 Lynx routes 8, 38, 42; I-Ride

METROPOLIS

Metropolis boasts a 13ft (4m) video wall and Moulin-Rouge-meets-Victoriana decor. It plays dance classics from the '80s to current hits. Over 18s only.

✚ F7 ✉ Pointe*Orlando, 9101 International Drive ☎ 407/370-3700 🕐 Thu–Sun 9am–2am 🚌 Lynx routes 8, 38, 42; I-Ride

IS THAT REALLY YOU?

The legal age for drinking alcohol in the USA is 21 and this is stringently enforced. If you are 21–25, or are of legal age but look younger, always carry photo ID with you to enjoy a refreshing glass of beer or wine with dinner, or at a bar or club.

Dinner Shows

THE BLACK STALLION

You'll be entranced by the Black Stallion when he appears in performances of Arabian Nights. The character is a famous fictional equine hero in the books by Walter Farley and is well known around the world. Farley wrote 21 titles in all and The Black Stallion carries on in modern tales written by his son.

ARABIAN NIGHTS

The romance between Princess Sheherazade and her beau Prince Khalid is the story told by well-choreographed feats of horsemanship.
🕇 D11 ✉ 6225 West Irlo Bronson Highway, Kissimmee ☎ 407/397-2378 ⏰ Nightly 🚌 Lynx routes 55 and 56

CAPONE'S DINNER AND SHOW

Step back in time to the 1930s gangland Chicago for a "speakeasy"-style musical revue.
🕇 Off map ✉ 4740 West Irlo Bronson Highway, Kissimmee ☎ 401/397-2378 or 800/220-8428 ⏰ Shows nightly, times vary 🚌 Lynx routes 55 and 56

DOLLY PARTON'S DIXIE STAMPEDE

Lots of rodeo riding, animal racing and an "all-American" finale in this all-action show. Visit the show horses in their stables 9am–5pm.
🕇 F9 ✉ 8251 Vineland Road ☎ 407/238-4455 or 866/443-4943 ⏰ Shows at 6.30pm and 8.30pm 🚌 Lynx route 42

FIASCO'S CIRCUS AND MAGIC DINNER SHOW

A slapstick evening is in store as the staff disrupt your meal with practical jokes and circus tricks.
🕇 G6 ✉ 7430 Universal Boulevard, Orlando ☎ 407/226-7220 or 1 866/660-4272 ⏰ Nightly at 6.30pm 🚌 Lynx route 21; I-Ride

HOOP-DEE-DO MUSICAL REVUE

A Wild West jamboree with banjo-toting cowboys at a campfire singsong.
🕇 C8 ✉ Pioneer Hall, Disney's Fort Wilderness Resort ☎ 407/939-3463 ⏰ Seating at 5pm, 7.30pm and 9.30pm 🚌 Lynx route 302

MAKAHIKI LUAU

Traditional South Sea islands dances and music accompany a Pacific-style buffet.
🕇 F/G8 ✉ SeaWorld, 7007 SeaWorld Drive ☎ 1 800/327-2420 or 407/351-3600 ⏰ Nightly at 6.30pm 🚌 Lynx routes 8 and 50

MEDIEVAL TIMES

Knights on stallions joust to be "King's Champion." The Museum of Medieval Life opens 4pm daily.
🕇 Off map ✉ 4510 W. Irlo Bronson Highway, Kissimmee ☎ 407/396-2900 ⏰ Nightly – times differ by season 🚌 Lynx routes 55 and 56

PIRATE'S DINNER ADVENTURE

A swashbuckling yarn taking place around an impressive galleon set.
🕇 F6 ✉ 6400 Carrier Drive ☎ 407/248-0590 or 1 800/866-2469 ⏰ Nightly 8.30pm, sometimes 6.30pm show 🚌 Lynx routes 8, 38, 42; I-Ride

SLEUTH'S MERRY MYSTERY DINNER SHOW

What's there to do when one of the audience is murdered during the meal but to help to solve the crime. It's "Murder She Wrote" meets "Miss Marple."
🕇 F6 ✉ 7508 Universal Boulevard ☎ 407/363-1985 ⏰ Nightly 7.30pm, other shows depending on season 🚌 Lynx route 21; I-Ride

Bars

BIG RIVER GRILLE AND BREWING WORKS

This microbrewery and eatery offers an inside view into how beer is made. Casual dining.

➕ C10 ✉ Disney's BoardWalk, Epcot Resorts Boulevard ☎ 407/939-5100 ⏰ Daily 11am–2am 🚌 Lynx route 303

THE GLOBE

One of the bars and restaurants that make up Wall Street Plaza, the Globe offers sushi and live music to accompany early evening drinks. Patio for warm evenings.

➕ K3 ✉ Wall Street ☎ 407/849-9904 ⏰ Daily 11am–2pm 🚌 Lynx routes 3, 6, 7, 11, 13, 18, 51 and 200

HOWL AT THE MOON

Lively bar where clients are encouraged to sing along to the recorded music or piano players.

➕ J3 ✉ 55 West Church Street ☎ 407/841-4695 ⏰ 4pm–2am 🚌 Lynx route 20

LATITUDES

A roof-top bar makes this one of the most popular venues in the downtown area. It turns into an evening venue, playing the latest chart sounds.

➕ J3 ✉ 33 West Church Street ☎ 407/649-4270 ⏰ Mon–Wed 3pm–10pm, Thu–Sun 3pm–2am 🚌 Lynx routes 20, 22, 36 and 40

MARGARITAVILLE

A little corner of the Bahamas in Orlando, Margaritaville has patios and balconies for you to soak up the sunshine and a cocktail. Jimmy Buffet's tunes offer a lilting sound track.

➕ F6 ✉ CityWalk, 6000 Universal Boulevard ☎ 407/224-2155 ⏰ Nightly 11am–2am 🚌 Lynx routes 21, 37, 40

MOTOWN CAFÉ

This Motown music-themed establishment features a great bar and restaurant. You'll be able to hear all your favorites, from Stevie Wonder to the Supremes, and view lots of memorabilia.

➕ F6 ✉ CityWalk, 1000 Universal Plaza ☎ 407/363-8000 ⏰ Daily 11am–2am 🚌 Lynx route 303

MULVANEY'S

The most popular Irish bar in the downtown area, with imported draft beers and live music.

➕ J3 ✉ 27 West Church Street ☎ 407/872-3296 ⏰ Daily 11am–2am 🚌 Lynx route 20

PAT O'BRIEN'S

Pat O'Brien opened his bar in Bourbon Street, New Orleans in 1933. His "Hurricane" cocktail soon made it famous. Pat O'Brien's at CityWalk brings the Big Easy to Orlando. It's Mardi Gras all year here.

➕ F6 ✉ CityWalk ☎ 407/224-2106 ⏰ Nightly 4pm–2am 🚌 Lynx routes 21, 37 and 40

ROCK N ROLL BEACH CLUB

There's beer, pool, games and live rock bands at this Disney tribute to the beer hall.

➕ D/E9 ✉ Pleasure Island, Downtown Disney, 1590 Buena Vista Drive, Lake Buena Vista ☎ 407/828-3025 ⏰ Nightly 7pm–2am 🚌 Lynx routes 300, 301, 302, 303 and 304

COCKTAILS

Cocktails are an integral part of the party scene in Orlando, so you'll need to get the lowdown on what to order.

Daiquiri – Jamaica rum, lime and powdered sugar
Margarita – tequila, triple sec and a dash of lime juice
Martini – vodka or gin with a dash of vermouth
Pina Colada – light rum, pineapple juice and coconut cream
Tequila Sunrise – tequila, orange juice and cranberry juice

83

Cinema

HOLLYWOOD STATISTICS

With Hollywood the major player in filmmaking it's not surprising that a trip to the movies is one of the most popular ways in America to spend a Saturday night. In the weekend April 15–17 2005 over $68 million dollars was spent at the box office. To date, the highest grossing film in American and world box offices is *Titanic*, while the film that made the most money during its first weekend was *Spider-Man 2*. What's coming next to a theater near you?

ALOMA CINEMA GRILL

As the name suggests, Aloma serves food during the performances making for a different viewing atmosphere. It allows smoking in the two auditoria.
🚇 L1 ✉ 2155 Aloma Avenue, Winter Park ☎ 407/678-8214
🎬 Showings 1pm–9pm
🚌 Lynx route 13

AMC CELEBRATION

1950s-style cinema with two theaters showing the latest releases. Movie going as it used to be.
🚇 Off map ✉ Front Street, Celebration ☎ 407/566-1403
🎬 Showings around 5pm, 7pm

AMC PLEASURE ISLAND 24

A 24-screen complex showing top 20 recent releases.
🚇 D/E9 ✉ Downtown Disney, 1500 Buena Vista Drive, Lake Buena Vista ☎ 407/298-4488
🎬 Showings 12.30–10.30
🚌 Lynx routes 300, 301, 302, 303 and 304

CINEMARK FESTIVAL BAY

Multiscreen complex showing the latest releases.
🚇 G6 ✉ 5150 International Drive ☎ 407/351-3117
🎬 Showings noon–10.30
🚌 Lynx 8, 24 and 42; I-Ride

DOWNTOWN MEDIA ARTS CENTER

The 80-seat digital cinema of this center shows independent and art-house films such as Oscar-nominated shorts.
🚇 K3 ✉ 39 South Magnolia Avenue ☎ 407/992-1200
🎬 Screenings 3pm–11pm

🚌 Lynx routes 3, 6, 7, 11, 13, 18, 51 and 200; Lymmo

ENZIAN THEATER

As Central Florida's only full-time, not-for-profit alternative cinema, Enzian exists to inspire, entertain, educate and connect the community through film of all genres, including foreign language. Also hosts the Florida Film Festival.
🚇 K3 ✉ 1300 South Orlando Avenue, Maitland ☎ 407/629-0054 or 407/629-1088
🎬 Showings Mon–Thu 6.30pm and 9.30pm, Fri–Sun 3.30pm, 6.30pm and 9.30pm 🚌 Lynx route 39

MUVICO POINTE 21 THEATERS

Twenty-one separate theaters in the Pointe* Orlando complex. The screen is six stories high and is unique in the city.
🚇 F7 ✉ Pointe*Orlando, 9101 International Drive ☎ 407/926-6843 🎬 Showings 11am–11pm
🚌 Lynx routes 8, 38, 42; I-Ride

REGAL WINTER PARK STADIUM

Multiscreen complex close to the center of Winter Park.
🚇 K1 ✉ Orlando Avenue, Winter Park ☎ 407/628-0035
🎬 Showings noon–11pm
🚌 Lynx routes 1 and 9

UNIVERSAL CINEPLEX

The only multicinema complex to offer beer and wine to enhance your viewing pleasure. Multiscreens offer the latest popular choices.
🚇 F6 ✉ CityWalk ☎ 407/354-5998 or 354-3374
🎬 Showings noon–11pm
🚌 Lynx routes 21, 37 and 40

Theater and the Classics

HELEN STAIRS THEATER

Built in the 1920s and refurbished in the late 1990s, the theater, home to the Helen Stairs Repertory group, stages a varied program.

➕ Off map ✉ 203 South Magnolia Avenue, Sanford ☎ 407/321-8111 🎟 Ticket office Mon–Fri 10am–4pm 🚌 Lynx route 34

MAD COW THEATER

This award-winning, avant garde company produces thought-provoking performances.

➕ K3 ✉ 105 East Pine Street ☎ 407/297-8788 🎟 Through the year 🚌 Lynx routes 3, 6, 7, 11, 13, 18, 51 and 200; Lymmo

ORLANDO BLACK ESSENTIAL THEATER

In the refurbished 1884 Church Street Theater, this group shares space with the Orlando Youth Theater to put on a varied program exploring the Afro-Caribbean community.

➕ J3 ✉ 110 West Church Street ☎ 407/491-9762 🎟 Performances throughout the year 🚌 Lynx route 20

ORLANDO OPERA

This company performs several productions each year and brings the classics to local schools.

➕ K2 ✉ Dr. Phillips Center for the Performing Arts, 1111 North Orange Avenue ☎ 407/426-1700 🎟 Throughout the year

ORLANDO PHILHARMONIC ORCHESTRA

The 80 musicians of Central Florida's orchestra perform at venues in the region.

➕ K2 ✉ 812 East Rollins Street ☎ 407/896-6700 🎟 100 performances yearly

ORLANDO-UNIVERSITY OF CENTRAL FLORIDA SHAKESPEARE FESTIVAL

Home to the only professional classical theater group in the city. Year-round performances of Shakespeare classics.

➕ K2 ✉ John and Rita Lowndes Shakespeare Theater, 812 East Rollins Street, Loch Haven Park ☎ 407/447-1700 🎟 Throughout the year 🚌 Lynx routes 1, 9 and 39

OVAL ON ORANGE

This artists' cooperative has studio and gallery space. Watch artists at work, view exhibitions and buy on-site.

➕ K3 ✉ 29 South Orange Avenue ☎ 407/648-1819 🎟 Thu 11am–2pm, Fri 11am–10pm, Sat 3pm–10pm 🚌 Lynx routes 3, 6, 7, 11, 13, 18, 51 and 200; Lymmo

ROLLINS COLLEGE

An annual program of dance, music, theater and film. Bach Festival concerts are a highlight.

➕ L1 ✉ 1000 Holt Avenue, Winter Park ☎ 407/646-2256 🎟 Throughout the year 🚌 Lynx routes 1, 9 and 23

SOUTHERN BALLET THEATER

Orlando's professional ballet company has 25 dancers performing classical and modern ballets and repertoire.

➕ K2 ✉ Dr. Phillips Center for the Performing Arts, 1111 North Orange Avenue ☎ 407/426-1733 🎟 May–Oct

THE BOB CARR PERFORMING ARTS CENTER

Orlando's premier arts venue hosts orchestral, ballet and opera performances from the city's companies and a full program of touring seasons and concerts (✉ 401 West Livingston Street ☎ 407/849-2577, box office 497/849-2020 🎟 Box office open Mon–Fri 10am–5pm and 3 hours before performances). Tickets for most city arts performances can be bought from Ticketmaster outlets or ☎ 407/839-3900, www.ticketmaster.com

Budget Hotels

PRICES

Luxury — more than $275
Mid-range — $150–$275
Budget — less than $150

DISNEY ALL-STAR RESORTS

This vast motel-style property has three themes: sports, movies and music. Each of the 5,700 rooms is a self-contained unit. Food court, pool, laundry and shuttles to Disney parks.
✚ B10/11 ✉ 1701 West Buena Vista Drive, Lake Buena Vista ☎ 407/939-5000, fax 407/939-7333, www.disney.go.com 🚌 Lynx route 302

DISNEY POP CENTURY RESORTS

Pop Century is a large motel-style property with 2,800 units and shuttles to Disney parks.
✚ C10/11 ✉ 1050 Century Drive, off Victory Way, Lake Buena Vista ☎ 407/938-4000, fax 407/938-4040, www.disney.go.com 🚌 Lynx route 301

HAWTHORN SUITES

Comfortable one- and two-bedroom studios with kitchens are good value. Pool, plus shuttles to Disney parks.
✚ F8 ✉ 6435 Westwood Boulevard ☎ 407/351-6600 or 800/527-1133, fax 407/351-1977, www.hawthorn.com 🚌 Lynx route 42; I-Ride

QUALITY SUITES MAINGATE EAST

Good family hotel with one- and two-bedroom suites. Buffet breakfast is included in the rate. The hotel is in walking distance of Old Town. Shuttles to main parks.
✚ D11 ✉ 5876 West Irlo Bronson Highway, Kissimmee ☎ 407/396-8040 or 877/424-6423, fax 407/396-6766, www.choicehotels.com 🚌 Lynx routes 58 and 56

SERALAGO HOTEL AND SUITES

Recently refurbished family resort with pools, playgrounds and tennis. Kid's Suites with small kitchen allow families to sleep in one unit. All 614 rooms have a fridge. Shuttle to Disney parks.
✚ E11 ✉ 5678 Irlo Bronson Highway, Kissimmee ☎ 407/396-4488, fax 407/396-8915 🚌 Lynx routes 55 and 56

SHERATON STUDIO CITY HOTEL

This tall tower hotel is a landmark on I-Drive. It has art deco decor and each of the 302 spacious rooms has a fridge.
✚ F6 ✉ 5905 International Drive ☎ 407/351-2100, fax 407/345-5249, www.starwoodhotels.com 🚌 Lynx routes 8, 38 and 42; I-Ride

SIERRA SUITES ORLANDO

Suites with sleeping, cooking and sitting areas, plus a large pool, make the Sierra good value. Eateries close by.
✚ E9 ✉ 8100 Palm Parkway, Lake Buena Vista ☎ 407/239-4300, fax 407/239-4446, www.sierrasuites.com 🚌 Lynx route 300

THE VERANDA BED AND BREAKFAST

European-style bed-and-breakfast set in a wonderful group of renovated mansions. The 12 rooms are individually furnished. There's a pool and spa. Breakfast is included.
✚ K3 ✉ 115 Summerlin Road ☎ 407/845-0321 www.theverandabandb.com 🚌 Lynx routes 5, 15 and 39

Mid-Range Hotels

CELEBRATION HOTEL

This clapboard boutique hotel, with 115 rooms, sits on the lakeside at Celebration with shopping and dining on the doorstep. Shuttles to Disney parks.

✚ Off map ✉ 700 Bloom Street ☎ 407/556-6000 or 888/499-3800, fax 407/566-1884, www.celebrationhotel.com

CROWN PLAZA UNIVERSAL

One block from I-Drive, the Crown Plaza is both a tourist and a business hotel, with pool, fitness room and laundry. Shuttle service to Disney and Universal.

✚ G6 ✉ 7800 Universal Boulevard ☎ 407/355-0550 or 1 800/294-0946, fax 407/355-0504, www.crownplazauniversal.com 🚌 Lynx route 21; I-Ride

DISNEY'S CONTEMPORARY RESORT

The Contemporary is set on the Disney monorail and has fine facilities for families, including child-care. Transport to Disney parks is good.

✚ B8 ✉ 4600 North World Drive, Lake Buena ☎ 407/824-1000 or 407/939-6244, fax 407/824-3539, www.disney.go.com 🚌 Lynx routes 50, 56 and 302

DISNEY'S CORONADO SPRINGS RESORT

The Coronado's 1,900 guest rooms sit around a natural lake. The food court offers a range of dining for families.

✚ B10 ✉ 1000 West Buena Vista Drive, Lake Buena Vista ☎ 407/939-1000, fax 407/939-1001, www.disney.go.com 🚌 Lynx route 303

DOUBLETREE CASTLE HOTEL

Castle Hotel's turrets make it easy to find as you stroll down I-Drive. The medieval theme continues in the decor of the 216 rooms. Shuttle to all major theme parks.

✚ F7 ✉ 8629 International Drive ☎ 407/345-1511 or 800/952-7285, fax 407/248-8181 🚌 Lynx routes 8, 38, 42; I-Ride

MARRIOTT IMPERIAL PALM VILLAS

The 46 one- or two-bedroom apartments of the Palm Villas make it a cozy place to stay. It's within walking distance of cafés and restaurants.

✚ E10 ✉ 8404 Vacation Way ☎ 1 407/238-6200, fax 407/238-6247, www.marriott.com 🚌 Lynx route 300

PARK PLAZA HOTEL

In the heart of Winter Park, this intimate hotel harks back to an earlier era. Rooms are individually furnished.

✚ L1 ✉ 307 Park Avenue South, Winter Park ☎ 407/647-1072, fax 407/647-4081 🚌 Lynx routes 1, 9 and 39

RENAISSANCE ORLANDO SEAWORLD RESORT

The Olympic-size pool is the obvious feature of this large hotel, which also has a golf course. The 778 rooms are well furnished. Those at the front get good views of nightly SeaWorld fireworks display.

✚ F8 ✉ 6677 Sea Harbor Drive ☎ 407/351-5555 or 800/327-6677, fax 407/351-9991, www.marriott.com 🚌 Lynx routes 8 and 50; I-Ride

WHAT'S THAT STRANGE NOISE?

The atrium of the Renaissance Orlando SeaWorld Resort is home to some unusual creatures. In the aviary you'll find kookaburras, members of the kingfisher family and native to Australia.

The birds live in forest woodland and bush land, eating lizards, snakes and insects. They have a unique loud "laughing" call that can be heard echoing around the hotel from time to time.

Luxury Hotels

SAVE WITH THE MAGICARD

The Orlando MagiCard offers a range of visitor benefits, including discounts on many attractions. The major cost saving comes in the accommodation section, with hotels in various price ranges offering discount to card members. This must be booked before arriving in Orlando, so download the MagiCard from the Convention and Visitors Bureau website at **www.orlandoinfo.com**

DISNEY'S GRAND FLORIDIAN SPA RESORT

The flagship of Disney's portfolio, the Grand Floridian has sandy beaches on the Seven Seas Lagoon. There are restaurants and a spa.
➕ B8 ✉ 4401 Grand Floridian Drive ☎ 407/824-3000, fax 407/824-3186, www.disney.go.com 🚌 Lynx route 302

DISNEY'S YACHT AND BEACH CLUB RESORT

Two resorts in one, the lakeside clubs have the theme of the seaside villages of America's northeast. Rooms have 24-hour room service.
➕ C9 ✉ 1700–1800 Epcot Resort Boulevard ☎ 407/934-8000, fax 407/934-3450, www.disney.go.com 🚌 Lynx route 303

HARD ROCK HOTEL

This Universal hotel has rock memorabilia worth $1 million, though the rooms are subdued. You can walk to Universal parks; free transport to SeaWorld, Discovery Cove and Wet 'n' Wild.
➕ F6 ✉ 5800 Universal Boulevard ☎ 407/503-7625, www.universalorlando.com 🚌 Lynx routes 12, 37 and 40

HYATT REGENCY-GRAND CYPRESS

A grand hotel anchored by a Jack Nicklaus-designed golf course. There's also an amazing pool, restaurants and a spa. Elegant rooms have private terraces.
➕ E9 ✉ 1 Grand Cypress Boulevard, off route 535 ☎ 407/239-1234 or 800/233-1234, www.hyatt.com

PEABODY ORLANDO

Probably I-Drive's most sophisticated hotel, the Peabody is a high-rise haven with plush rooms and the excitement of the Peabody ducks.
➕ F7 ✉ 9810 International Drive ☎ 407/352-4000 or 800/PEA-BODY (732-2639) 🚌 Lynx routes 8, 38, 42; I-Ride

PORTOFINO BAY

Portofino Bay, styled as a Mediterranean seaside village, has waterside walkways and themed restaurants. Walking distance to Universal parks, free transport to SeaWorld, Discovery Cove and Wet 'n' Wild.
➕ F6 ✉ 5600 Universal Boulevard ☎ 407/503-1000 www.loewshotels.com 🚌 Lynx routes 12, 37 and 40

RITZ CARLTON GRANDE LAKES

Set in 5,000 acres (2,020 ha) of lush grounds, the Ritz Carlton offers 584 luxurious rooms, a spa and a highly regarded golf course.
➕ H8 ✉ 4040 Central Florida Parkway ☎ 407/206-1100, www.grandelakes.com 🚌 Lynx route 43

WESTIN GRAND BOHEMIAN

From this luxurious downtown hotel you can reach the city's best bars on foot. Rooms boast Heavenly Beds. There's a rooftop pool and 24-hour room service.
➕ K3 ✉ 325 South Orange Avenue ☎ 407/313-9000, fax 407/313-9001, www.starwoodhotels.com 🚌 Lynx routes 3, 6, 7, 11, 13, 18, 51 and 200; Lymmo route

ORLANDO
travel facts

Essential Facts

Electricity
- The power supply is 110/120 volts AC (60 cycles).
- A transformer is needed for 240-volt electrical equipment.

Etiquette
- Queuing is the norm.
- Tipping is expected for services.
- Topless sunbathing is forbidden.
- Smoking is restricted or forbidden at all attractions.
- Some upscale resorts and restaurants have a dress code.

Lone and women travelers
Most hotels don't charge a single person occupancy supplement. There is little fear of being hassled. Bear in mind the advice given under sensible precautions (▶ 93).

Money matters
- The best place to exchange non-US currency is at a bank.
- US dollar traveler's checks are the most secure way to carry money and they are accepted as cash in most places.
- US dollars can be obtained from Automatic Teller Machines (ATMs) with either credit or debit cards if you have a Personal Identification Number (PIN).
- ATMs are plentiful (found at banks, but also shopping malls, attractions and gas stations). Some charge an extra fee for their use.
- Credit cards are universally accepted. Automatic payment machines, such as in gas stations, may not accept foreign cards.

National holidays
- Jan 1: New Year's Day
- Third Mon Jan: Martin Luther King Day
- Third Mon Feb: Presidents' Day
- Mar/Apr: Easter
- Last Mon May: Memorial Day
- Jul 4: Independence Day
- First Mon Sep: Labor Day
- Second Mon Oct: Columbus Day
- Nov 11: Veterans' Day
- Fourth Thu Nov: Thanksgiving
- Dec 25: Christmas Day
- Boxing Day (Dec 26): is not a public holiday in the US. Some stores open on national holidays.

Opening hours
- Stores: most independent stores open Mon–Sat 9–5.30 or 9–7.
- Malls: usually open Mon–Sat 10–9 and Sun noon–6.
- Banks: larger branches may have a drive-through service on Sat 8–noon.
- Post offices: Mon–Fri 9–5, some open longer weekdays and Sat 9–noon.
- Museums: hours vary but core hours are 10–5.
- Theme parks: theme park hours vary seasonally and daily. Core winter hours 10–5; core summer hours 9–8.

Places of worship
There are churches of many denominations in Orlando. Consult the telephone directory or the official tourist office in Orlando ✉ 8723 International Drive ☎ 407/363-5872.

Student travelers
- Most hotel rooms sleep 4 (in 2 queen beds), so rates work well for groups of travelers.
- There is one hostel in Orlando, Palm Lakefront Resort and Hostel ✉ 4840 West Irlo Bronson Highway (Highway 192), Kissimmee ☎ 407/396-1759.
- Some museums offer discounts for student visitors.

Time differences
- Florida is mainly on Eastern Standard Time (GMT -5).
- The Panhandle region, west of the Apalachicola River, is on Central Standard Time (GMT -6).

Toilets
- The cleanest and safest restrooms are in hotels, convenience stores and shopping malls.
- All attractions have good facilities.

Tourist offices
The only official tourist office in Orlando is found at
✉ 8723 International Drive, Orlando FL 32819
☎ 407/363-5872
Staff can send information before your trip and help during your stay.

GETTING AROUND

- Orlando has a good public bus system, Lynx, but the distances involved can mean long journey times and the timetables to Walt Disney World® Resorts make it impractical for tourist use.
- The system runs daily 4am–2am, with reduced services on holidays.
- Services must be accessed from a Lynx bus stop; look for a round emblem of a lynx footprint.
- Signs correspond to the color of the particular route or "link."
- The transport authority also runs Lymmo, a free circular bus service that links downtown areas with the Lynx Central Station and venues near the Bob Carr Center.
- It runs every 5 minutes during office hours, 10–15 minutes at other times.
Contact details:
Lynx Central Station
✉ 455 North Garland Avenue
☎ 407/841-5969, www.golynx.com

- The I-Ride trolleybus links attractions along International Drive. It operates 8am–10.30pm every day. It can be accessed from numbered stops along its routes.
- Contact details: ☎ 407/354-5656.

Where to get maps
- Lynx: get route maps from all terminus offices or the Orlando/Orange County Convention and Visitors Bureau office at ✉ 8723 International Drive.
- I-Ride: from the Orlando/Orange County Convention and Visitors Bureau and hotels where passes are sold.

Discounts/types of tickets
- Lynx: tickets cost $1.50 and are valid for 90 minutes from first use.
- Day passes (valid from 4am on the day of use to 3am the following morning) cost $3, and a seven-day pass is $10.
- Seniors and disabled travelers benefit from reduced fares.
- Single fare and day passes are available on the bus (cash only, no change given). Other passes are available at Lynx offices, and some supermarkets and shops (see website or Lynx route map).
- I-Ride: single fares are .75c, seniors' cost .25c and under 12s' free. Drivers don't offer change.
- Day passes cost $3 per person, 3-day passes $5, 5-day passes $7, 7-day passes $9 and 14-day passes $16. Passes are sold at the Tourist Office and at hotels and shops.

Taxis
- Official taxis are painted yellow with the word TAXI on the sides and a lighted sign on the roof.
- Taxi stands can be found outside all attractions, major hotels and airport arrival terminals.

91

- All hotels and most restaurants will be happy to call a taxi for you.
- Taxis will have a meter and rates will be posted inside. Make sure that the meter is set correctly for the location and the time of day.
- Never use an unofficial taxi.

MEDIA & COMMUNICATIONS

Mailing a letter/postcard

- Post offices: US post offices are usually open Mon–Fri 9–5, but are not always in obvious locations. For International Drive there is a post office at ✉ Mall at Millennia.
- Vending machines sell stamps but at a 25 percent premium.
- Hotels and most major attractions often provide postal services.

Telephones

- Most hotels have international and local dialing. Local calls will be free or cheap; long-distance and international calls attract a premium. For these use a low-cost provider such as AT&T who will issue you an access number.
- Prepaid phone cards are sold at drugstores and visitor centers. Calls are charged at a fixed rate.
- Public telephones are plentiful. These operate with cash, credit cards or calling cards and can be used for long-distance and international calls.
- From public phones dial 0 for the operator. Dial 1 plus the area code for numbers within the US and Canada. Dial 411 to find US and Canadian numbers.

International dialing codes

- Dial 011 followed by
- UK: 44
- Ireland: 353
- Australia: 61

Newspapers and magazines

- The *Orlando Sentinel* is the main local daily with national news and international headlines.
- *USA Today* is the most widely read daily national. It is available at hotel reception desks and from self-service vending machines.
- English and other European newspapers can be bought at Cyber Shack Café ✉ 6438 International Drive, and at Street Corner News ✉ Florida Mall.

Radio and television

- There are numerous commercial television stations and most hotels offer 20–30 channels.
- Local stations providing programming and news are WESH and FOX 35.
- Radio is a commercialized arena, so simply tune your dial to the music/talk station you like.

EMERGENCIES

- Dial 911 to access all the emergency services. Explain your circumstances and location to the operator and the appropriate service will be dispatched.

Embassies and consulates

- British Vice-Consul ✉ Suite 2110, SunTrust Center, 200 South Orange Avenue, Orlando ☎ 407/581-1540.
- British Embassy ✉ 3100 Massachusetts Avenue, Washington DC ☎ 202/588-7800.
- German Embassy ✉ 4645 Reservoir Road, Washington DC ☎ 202/298-4000.
- Canadian Embassy ✉ 501 Pennsylvania Avenue North West, Washington DC ☎ 202/682-1740.
- Eire ✉ 2234 Massachusetts Avenue North West, Washington DC ☎ 202/462-3939.

- Australia ✉ 1601 Massachusetts Avenue North West, Washington DC ☎ 202/979-3000.
- New Zealand ✉ 37 Observatory Circle North West, Washington DC ☎ 202/328-4800.

Lost property

- Check with the front desk at your hotel.
- Public transport, taxi firms and all tourist attractions will have a lost property department.
- Report all stolen or lost credit cards immediately.
- You will need a police report to make an insurance claim on your return home.

Medical treatment

- There are charges for all medical treatment in the US, therefore it is imperative that visitors have insurance that covers any unforeseen medical problems. Look for policies with a minimum $5,000,000 limit.
- Quality of facilities and staff expertise is extremely high.
- Full service hospital ✉ 601 East Rollins Road ☎ 407/303-6611.
- Walk-in medical center at ✉ 6001 Vineland Road, Suite 108 ☎ 407/351-6682 (close to Universal Studios) and ✉ 12500 South Apopka Vineland Road (SR 535) ☎ 407/934-2273 (close to the Disney parks).
- All major attractions will have good first aid stations to help with major and minor incidents. Ask a member of staff for help.

Medicines

- Pharmacies stock a wide range of medicines available without prescription.
- Pharmacies must employ a qualified pharmacist who can advise on a range of minor ailments and suggest suitable treatments.

Sensible precautions

- High temperatures can cause dehydration. Keep fluid levels up and avoid too much coffee and alcohol.
- The Florida sun is very strong. Wear a hat, cover arms and legs and use a strong sunscreen.
- This advice applies even more strongly for children. They get dehydrated or suffer sunstroke more quickly than adults.
- Feet are prone to blisters during long days at parks. Wear comfortable shoes and carry bandaids to cover pressure points.
- Mosquitoes can be a nuisance at places such as National Parks. Apply a good repellent and keep arms covered.
- Ticks can carry disease. During summer months check for bites after you've walked or hiked in the backwoods and see a doctor if you find evidence of bites. Don't attempt to remove a tick yourself.
- Make a copy of travel tickets, itinerary and important items like passport number and credit card numbers. Keep these separate from your genuine documents.
- Beware of carrying expensive items such as jewelry or cameras.
- Don't carry large amounts of cash.
- Don't leave anything of value in your car and make sure nothing is on show when you park it.
- At night, drive on well-lit streets. Walk in well-lit busy streets.
- If in doubt, take taxis rather than walking into unfamiliar territory.
- Don't give your hotel room number to anyone.
- Always verify the identity of any-one who calls at your hotel room.

Index

CityPack
Orlando *Top 25*

Written by Lindsay Bennett **Cover Design** Tigist Getachew Fabrizio La Roca

A CIP catalogue record for this book is available from the British Library.

ISBN-10: 0 7495 4748 0
ISBN-13: 978-0-7495-4748-6

Published by AA Publishing, a trading name of Automobile Association Developments Limited, whose registered office is Fanum House, Basingstoke, Hampshire RG21 4EA. Registered number 1878835.

© **AUTOMOBILE ASSOCIATION DEVELOPMENTS LIMITED** 2005
First published 2005
Colour separation by Keenes, Andover, UK.
Printed and bound by Hang Tai D&P Limited, Hong Kong.

ACKNOWLEDGEMENTS
The Automobile Association would like to thank the following photographers, libraries and associations for their assistance in the preparation of this book:
Boggy Creek Airboat Rides 50t, 50c, 57; **Busch Gardens, Tampa Bay** back cover, **Montu**, 20tc, 20b, 51t; © **Disney** 26, 27, 28, 29, 31, 33t; **Getty Images** 16cl (Hulton Archive); **The Charles Hosmer Morse Museum of American Art** 48t; **Harry P. Leu Gardens/Orlando** 47t, 47c; **Orlando Museum of Art** 46t, 46b; **Orlando Science Center** 45t, 45c; **Photodisc** 239; **Rex Features Ltd** 17; **SeaWorld Orlando & Discovery Cove** front cover **Skytower, girl at Discovery Cove; Stockbyte** 5t; © **Universal Orlando** front cover globe, **Dueling Dragons Ride**, 37t, 51b, 53, 54; **Wet 'n' Wild, Orlando** front cover **The Blast,** front cover background **The Flyer; WonderWorks, Orlando** 35b
The remaining pictures are held in the Association's own library (AA WORLD TRAVEL LIBRARY) and were taken by the following photographers: **Pete Bennett** front cover astronaut, back cover CityWalk sign, Nascar restaurant, Live Music sign, 1t, 2t, 4t, 6t, 7tl, 7tc, 7tr, 8tl, 8bl, 8tc, 8bc, 8/9, 9bl, 9c, 9cr, 10c, 11tl, 11tr, 11c, 12c, 13, 14cl, 14cr, 15cl, 15cr, 18tr, 18cl, 18cr, 19tl, 19tc, 19cl, 19cr, 20tr, 21tl, 21tc, 21c, 22tr, 22c, 22b, 23cr, 23b, 24cl, 24cr, 25, 30t, 30b, 32t, 32b, 34, 35t, 36t, 36b, 37b, 38, 39t, 39b, 40t, 40c, 41, 42t, 42b, 43t, 43b, 44, 49t, 49c, 49b, 52t, 52c, 52b, 56, 58, 59, 60, 61, 63t, 63b, 89t, 89c, 89br; **Tony Souter** front cover flamingo, 1b, 9tr, 9br, 10t, 12t, 14t, 16t, 16cr, 18tl, 20tl, 22tl, 24t, 62, 89bc

A02378
Cover maps produced from map data supplied by Global Mapping, Brackley, UK. Copyright © Global Mapping. Sheet map supplied by Global Mapping, Brackley, UK. Copyright © Global Mapping Transport map © Communicarta Ltd., UK

TITLES IN THE CITYPACK SERIES
• Amsterdam • Bangkok • Barcelona • Beijing • Berlin • Boston • Brussels & Bruges • Chicago • Dublin • Florence • Hong Kong • Las Vegas • Lisbon • London • Los Angeles • Madrid • Melbourne • Miami • Milan •• Montréal • Munich • Naples • New York • Paris • Prague • Rome • San Francisco • Seattle • Shanghai • Singapore • Sydney • Tokyo • Toronto • Venice • Vienna • Washington DC •